Unlimited Progress

The Grand Delusion of the Modern World

DENNIS KNIGHT HEFFNER, M.D.

iUniverse, Inc.
New York   Bloomington

Unlimited Progress
The Grand Delusion of the Modern World

iUniverse books may be ordered through booksellers or by contacting:

iUniverse
1663 Liberty Drive
Bloomington, IN 47403
www.iuniverse.com
1-800-Authors (1-800-288-4677)

Because of the dynamic nature of the Internet, any Web addresses or
links contained in this book may have changed since publication and
may no longer be valid. The views expressed in this work are solely those
of the author and do not necessarily reflect the views of the publisher,
and the publisher hereby disclaims any responsibility for them.

ISBN: 978-1-4502-3785-7 (pbk)
ISBN: 978-1-4502-3786-4 (cloth)
ISBN: 978-1-4502-3787-1 (ebk)

Library of Congress Control Number: 2010908676

Printed in the United States of America

iUniverse rev. date: 7/7/2010

To my most favorite spouse,
Nola

And my most favorite daughter,
Lally

The toil of all that be,
Helps not the primal fault.
It rains into the sea,
And still the sea is salt.

A. E. Housman

Contents

Foreword

I congratulate Dr. Dennis Heffner on his writing this compelling and insightful book, after numerous years of sharing his ideas with Nola; Ron, my husband; and me. Dennis utilizes both cross-disciplinary and historical approaches to address society's current optimism of unlimited progress with a more practical and realistic perspective. Additionally, he appeals to individuals in Jeffersonian tradition, to take responsibility and exert their voices of commonsense judgment to address our leaders to act in a more pragmatic manner. I think his ideas and solutions are cogent and hopeful and will resonate with others.

With gratitude and best wishes,
Carol Zaremba Berg, Ph.D.
January 31, 2010

Preface

My college education was in engineering and physics. Subsequently, I went to medical school and my career has been in medicine (surgical pathology). Thus, politics is not my professional field. Nevertheless, some things I have perceived within the framework of science seem to me possibly to have some implication for political matters, and describing this implication is the aim of this book.

There are modern fields of study that include the word "science" but which are more closely related to the humanities than they are to conventional or formal science. Examples are political science and other social sciences. In this book, the word "science" is meant to refer to a more restricted conventional view of "hard" sciences, such as physics, chemistry, and biology. These are the sciences that have led to the technological revolutions vitally important to the development of the modern world; thus, they are hard sciences in that they have been the bedrock foundation for progress.

But the adjective "hard" has a more metaphorical meaning for this book. Some of the examples from science that I use as evidence for my assertions about progress are a bit hard to understand. Yet this abstruseness very much relates to the fundamental importance of the examples. Most other people have not recognized many of these examples, but they are factors of extensive and fundamental import within science and technology and, to a lesser but still significant extent, to more broad social issues. It is necessary for me to try to help the reader in understanding these examples in order to give them their due evidentiary weight. For the reader who must wrestle with some of these difficulties, my delving into complex scientific matters at least will serve one useful purpose. While some readers may disagree with some or most of my ideas and assertions, at least it should be evident that the thinking behind these ideas has not been just superficial or overly simplistic.

The modern-world delusion of unlimited progress that underlies the discussions in this book is "grand" in the following senses. It is grand because it is pervasive, persistent, and profound. Almost everyone shares in this delusion. It is grand because it is of extreme importance in contemporary worldviews. It is grand because it induces a giddy optimism. But this optimism is probably causing us to fly higher than we safely can. This giddy utopianism has become so extensive and pernicious that it is probably becoming perilous. It is now so ingrained in society that it may be intractable. But this book argues that we at least need to try to apply some brakes to this phenomenon. Otherwise, we may get our wings burned off as we try to approach closer to the sun.

D. Knight Heffner, M.D.
January 2010

Chapter 1

Progress Is a Percept Solely in the Modern Mind

Most of this book will focus on modern science and how it underlies and influences almost all of our general views about what the world is like. To emphasize this powerful effect of science and related technology on our worldviews, it may be helpful to briefly recount some aspects of how people perceived the world in ancient times before the influences of modern science came about. This will serve as a contrast to the modern perspective, and this contrast will highlight and emphasize the extent and strength of the influence science has had on general thinking about the world we live in. To begin, we will try to judge what the word "progress" may have meant to people in the ancient world.

The word "progress" has, not surprisingly, its roots in ancient language. In Latin, the prefix *pro* means "forward" and *gradi* means "to step or walk." But this literal meaning of forward walking connotes much less than the greatly expanded meaning that the word has today. There is reason to believe that in the ancient world the word mostly carried only the limited and literal meaning referring to mechanistic forward walking.

Of course, scholars will point out that there are numerous examples in the writings of Greek philosophers that seem to be related to a broader meaning of progress. But these examples seem to me to be mere snippets of progress and, overall, do not indicate very much of what in the modern world is conveyed by the word "progress."

A. Ancient Greece

Indeed, in pre-Socratic Greek philosophy, even the idea that there could be such a thing as real motion (e.g., forward walking) was problematic for some, and it was debatable whether reality was fixed or changing. Perhaps the perception of motion was illusory. Heraclitus and Parmenides had contrasting ideas about change and continuity. The former held that there indeed was change, so much so that "one could never step in the same river twice." Parmenides said that, although common sense might suggest that things change, this is an illusion. The world is complete and perfect and therefore cannot change. His pupil was Zeno, the founder of stoic philosophy, and he contrived three paradoxes of motion that are well known and to this day carry some import.

The most well known of these paradoxes is the one describing Achilles chasing a slower individual. Although Achilles was faster, there would be great difficulty in catching up to and surpassing the rival. Consider an example of a starting situation, with Achilles being one hundred yards behind the rival. As the race moves along, there will be a point at which Achilles has progressed to being only fifty yards behind, closing the distance by half. Then comes the point at which he has cut the fifty-yard trailing distance in half, to twenty-five yards. Then he cuts the twenty-five yards in half to twelve and a half yards. The obvious progression of the race is that for the remaining trailing distance, Achilles must continually cut that distance in half. But that will always mean that a remaining half persists to be reduced. This will continue *ad infinitum,* and thus Achilles will never be able to eliminate entirely a remaining trailing distance, let alone surpass the rival runner. Now, Zeno himself recognized that the conclusion was a contradiction to observation, but his argument was effective for his purpose, and the argument type was a logical one called *reductio ad absurdum.*

Of course, every modern person recognizes that this result is absurd, and therefore the argument is meaningless. But it is not so in the following way. To try to conversely argue that the story is wrong is a very formidable logical-mathematical challenge. Indeed, counterarguments did not approach cogency until the ideas of differential calculus with conceptions of infinitesimals were developed in the seventeenth century AD (CE). Even then it was problematic to compellingly demonstrate a counterargument. In recent decades there have been scientific (mathematical) articles discussing the challenging problem presented by Zeno's paradoxes. This is an example of the intractability of some philosophical problems that can persist from ancient times. Indeed, most of the major philosophical problems debated by ancient Greeks remain less than completely resolved to this day. The history of philosophy can be paraphrased as the "Long Debate" (Daniel N. Robinson). This by itself is some evidence that progress can be difficult and at least sometimes probably limited.

Regarding Greek philosophy and any ideas affecting the concept of progress, such ideas seem more oriented toward the concept of a stable world rather than a progressive one. Socrates argued that ethical truths were absolute and demonstrable, similar to the truths of geometry. Plato's fundamental view of the important world was one of ideal forms or essences. Yes, the visible, mundane world was one where things change, but these things were not as real and not as important as were the unchanging ideal forms.

Aristotle's ideas can be cited as perhaps including that of progress because of his thoughts in the area of *entelechy*, or teleological change. That is, change is viewed as aiming toward a goal or end. For example, a child changes (i.e., develops and matures) with the goal of becoming an adult. This certainly seems to imply an idea tantamount to progress. But I point out for our purposes that such ideas obviously entail a limit to the progress, the limit being the aim or goal toward which the progress is drawn. Overall and basically, Greek philosophy is much less underlain by ideas of progress than is our modern world.

B. ROMAN LAW

The development of the ancient Roman Empire would certainly seem to entail ideas of progress for those living within the empire. But some factors would tend to moderate such ideas.

The Greeks are known for great philosophical constructs. The Roman Empire grew upon some of these philosophical achievements, most notably in the realm of governance and the development of law. Indeed, followers of Zeno's stoicism were very important in developing such achievements. The Roman governance and laws came to produce a vast society lasting many centuries. It was mostly a relatively orderly society due to the effectiveness of Roman law. But it was a society governed by the few, and it is doubtful that the great majority of the populace sensed any significant progress during their individual lifetimes. Also, most individual lifetimes were shorter than they are today. This, combined with the absence of anything like the modern factors that spread education and societal information, surely meant that most people sensed nothing like progress. During the latter centuries of the empire, periods of debauchery and decline would hardly have been consistent with feelings of progress.

Over the longer term, the empire's spread can now be seen to have been limited, to have faltered at multiple points, and then of course to have collapsed in the fifth century AD (CE).

C. CYCLICAL HISTORY

So the ancient Western worlds that developed in Greece and the Roman Empire clearly were limited. This no doubt contributed to the subsequent views of many thinkers that history is cyclical. Vico (eighteenth century) and Spengler (twentieth century) are two such philosophers of history. Societies may progress, but the progress slows and even reverses. Even the late eighteenth and early nineteenth century historical philosophy of Hegel that included a type of advancement also included an Aristotelian end of such advancement. Likewise did the economic philosophy of Marx. A contemporary continuance of such thinking is found with Francis Fukuyama (*The End of History*). Throughout Western history, unlimited progress has not been a feature within scholarly thinking about history.

D. THE MEDIEVAL PERIOD

Any ideas about progress that some ancients may have had surely disappeared during the long Middle Ages. Although many events of course occurred during this extensive time, it is hard to suggest anything that might have engendered any sense of social progress. The long history of Scholasticism was one of looking backward to the ancient world as the model for what the world was like. Indeed, rather than progress, some things suggest that there was a pervasive idea that the real world was an aging one, much as individuals inexorably aged. Why would the world be otherwise? Judeo-Christian theology includes ideas of the end of times, the second coming of Christ, Armageddon, an apocalypse, and so on. The Mayan civilization is known for having some end-of-times concepts, as exemplified by the current film *2012*.

Consider the plague that devastated the population of Europe in the middle of the fourteenth century. It took 150 years for the population of this feudal society to recover. The population of mostly serfs did not have reason to believe in societal progress before this plague. Does it seem feasible that anyone had a conception of such progress during, or a century after, these times? Surely, the opposite must have been true.

In the beginning of the European Renaissance, there were glimmers of economic societal progress, with the incipient development of a mercantilism and a beginning of the development of a socioeconomic middle class. But the subsequent Age of Reason, the Enlightenment (circa 1700 to 1850), and the Industrial Revolution entailed progress that so completely overwhelmed any prior notions of societal advancement that it is within this modern age that we want to focus. Of course, the modern age includes the fantastic development of science and technology.

Although we so far have looked briefly at ancient and medieval societies, we subsequently will concentrate on the modern world and will claim that science and technology are the primary disciplines showing modern-world progress. But is this justified? Certainly modern society comprises much more than science and technology. Shouldn't progress be examined as a composite of all the complex aspects of our complex civilization? We will speak to these questions in the next chapter.

Chapter 2
The Two Cultures and the Science Wars

To properly paint the picture of progress, my focus is on science and technology. But this is only one side of modern development and progress. The other side comprises philosophy, literature, sociology, arts, religion, economics, and many other facets of the activities and endeavors of civilization that we will refer to as the humanities. This division is not always perfect or totally justified, but it will serve the purpose for making my points.

While societal progress in the humanities has occurred during modern times, with the exception of advances in economic goods and services, progress in the areas of the humanities is often difficult to perceive with certainty, document objectively, and quantitate or measure. Within science and technology, progress has often been so blatant, so profound, and so extensive that it gives most of the weight to the idea of progress in the modern world. Most of the economic progress we have made has been tied to technological progress, which in turn is usually based upon scientific progress. Also, scientific progress has, in a sense, "infected" society so much that it has contributed to, colored, and maybe even distorted perceptions of progress in the humanities, including socio-political areas. Therefore, when I later give evidence that progress is limited in science and technology, this limitation has import for the humanities and of course for political attitudes. Arguments for tempering irrational exuberance about progress in the scientific sphere implies a need for mitigating overenthusiastic ideas of progress in the humanities since ideas of progress in the latter have been influenced so much by progress in the sciences. In other words, if modern progress has been readily made in sciences but I can show that it is limited, this would suggest that, in other societal areas where progress has always been less readily made, progress is probably limited also, including politics and societal governance.

A.   THE TWO CULTURES

Before discussing the development of science, we should note that science before the modern era was not a discipline denoted by that word. The word "science" was not formally used for such endeavors until c. 1833 when William Whewell applied the word "scientist" to those already practicing what was by then a well-developed field. Before that time, scientific activities were generally referred to as natural philosophy. But we will use the word "science" to refer to activities throughout history that, in retrospect, would be appropriately labeled as such.

The differences between sciences and what would now be referred to as the humanities have been subtle throughout most of history, but there are traces of such dating back to ancient times. Plato's concentration on the importance of the ideal world of the heavens is a bit different from Aristotle's frequent involvement with more real-world matters (i.e., natural philosophy). There certainly are elements of early science within Aristotle's endeavors.

But it is in the early modern periods when such a two-sided division can be more clearly seen to develop. An important milestone in the development of modern science occurred four and a half centuries ago (AD 1543) with Copernicus's conception that Earth and the other planets revolved around the sun rather than Earth being the center of all things (i.e., center of the universe). It is probably not quite possible for contemporary people to really grasp what tumultuous shifts in thinking such a profound disruption in the worldview caused. Of course, it was so radical and so "impossible" that it was only very gradually adopted by the world's thinkers. The painstaking and very time-consuming gathering of data by Tycho Brahe on planetary positional changes and the subsequent use of these data by Johannes Kepler were early starts on the paths to confirming the Copernican Revolution. Kepler intuited that the data seemed to indicate elliptical orbits for the planets, including Earth, but even he remained dissatisfied with this possibility since he thought, as did everyone else, that the orbits should be perfect circles. (Ancient ideals remained strongly influential.) It was not until the seventeenth-century developments of Newtonian mechanics that the Copernican conception was compellingly completed. Overall, this was a sea change of progress in understanding the physical world.

Although Copernicus started things in 1543, it was not until shortly after 1600 that scientific thinking really gained some traction, and the scientific revolution usually is considered to date from this time (i.e., covering the last four centuries). It was in this first decade of the seventeenth century that Galileo developed his multiple telescopes. (The telescope was formally invented by another contemporary person, but Galileo certainly was the major developer of improvements of the early instrument.) It is in the friction between Galileo and the Catholic Church, despite Pope Urban VIII being a friend of Galileo, that we can see a definite tension between science and other human activities. In this case, religion is of course the other activity.

When Galileo first observed the four moons of Jupiter, this was a major step in confirming the world-shaking Copernican concept. Here was direct evidence of heavenly bodies revolving around something other than Earth. The moons could be seen as revolving around Jupiter. When Galileo attempted to show his evidence to others, including Church elders, many refused to be bothered even to look. Others claimed that what was being seen was some sort of "trick." In other words, maybe the spots being called moons were painted on the lenses or were otherwise somehow put into the telescope. No doubt Galileo tried to explain that since the moons shifted the same as the rest of the heavens when the telescope's viewing angle was shifted slightly on its axis, these "trick" explanations for the moons were not tenable. One can hardly imagine the probable extent of Galileo's frustration when others did not understand his explication. It was not understood because the naïve observers had no idea how the telescope worked. Galileo had constructed his instrument and of course knew its principles, but others (nonscientists) could not understand at all what they were seeing. They could not understand because they did not *do* what Galileo did. This is an example of the intractability of the gulf that can exist between one discipline and others.

Another development at this time was that of Francis Bacon, an Englishman who was contemporary with the Italian Galileo. Bacon's famous work was the *Novum Organum*, which means "a new instrument or method." This writing was a challenge to Aristotle's *Organon* and the entire medieval static scholasticism that appealed to the authority of ancient thinkers. Bacon argued that natural philosophy must be separated from theology. The new method was one of finding new knowledge through observing the particulars of the world. It was a method based upon experience and then progressing from the particulars of experience to useful generalizations—an inductive method. The knowledge based upon these generalizations could be useful for the betterment of mankind. Knowledge is power. Also, natural philosophy (science) was viewed as a dynamic, cooperative, cumulative enterprise. Science was viewed as being based upon evidence, the kind of evidence Galileo saw through his telescopes.

Bacon's argument for separating science from theology is one of a number of factors that eventually would result in the twentieth-century idea of a gulf between two cultures—the sciences and the humanities. Another factor can be seen in the reaction to eighteenth-century scientific enlightenment known as romanticism. This was instigated in the late eighteenth century by Rousseau and continued into the early nineteenth century, particularly in romantic literature and poetry. One very obvious example of the developing gulf can be seen in Mary Shelley's *Frankenstein*, a clear exposition of a type of adverse effect science might cause. Most readers will have heard of the Luddites' formation as a reaction to the adversities of the Industrial Revolution, the technological side of the fruits of science.

In the last half of the twentieth century, the gulf became more noteworthy to scholars. In 1959, a book by C. P. Snow titled *The Two Cultures and the Scientific Revolution* was published. The treatise emphasized the difference between two worldviews: (1) the sociology-constructivist view in which the scientific method is seen as very much embedded within and influenced by language and culture, and (2) the scientific viewpoint of the discipline being objective, unbiased, and based upon nonculturally influenced observations about nature. The phrase "two cultures" became shorthand for the rift (incomprehension tinged with hostility) between scientists and literary intellectuals. Although the controversies arising out of this rift were mostly evident only in academic intellectual circles and people outside the ivory towers were hardly aware of the skirmishes and battles, the problem is a profound and long-lasting one that sometimes can affect the world in practical ways.

B. THE SCIENCE WARS

The much-enhanced rift that became known as the science wars exemplifies the division that developed between the two cultures. This term has been used to refer to battles between the humanities and the sciences—or, roughly, between "postmodernists" and "realists"—that became pronounced in the 1990s. During this decade, the struggle even received some media attention. Social philosophies underlying this phenomenon, such as *postmodernism* and *deconstructionism,* are difficult concepts that I am not capable of trying to explain. But some factors underlying the emergence of the science wars are worth mentioning. One was the publication in 1962 of the book *The Structure of Scientific Revolutions* by Thomas Kuhn. The thesis maintained that the evolution of science is partly sociological, not simply based upon logical laws as was assumed by the philosophy of "logical positivism," which was so important in the first part of the twentieth century. This book seems to have underlain a period of increased questioning of the objectivity of science, with a consequent huge variety of critiques from within cultural anthropology, comparative literature, feminist studies, media studies, and so on.

One philosopher of science, S. L. Goldman, has denoted three additional factors that were important in leading to the science wars: (1) discussions of the "military-industrial complex," as begun by President Eisenhower in the late 1950s, with its influence upon the directions of science via corporate and government funding of science; (2) the aforementioned social-constructivist philosophies that underlay so much of academic humanistic endeavors and that tend to underplay the significance of, or even existence of, any objective reality; and (3) religious-creationist philosophy that became so prominent and influential in the 1990s.

The battlegrounds of the wars became more explicit in a number of publications and some large conferences in the 1990s. These included a 1994 book *Higher Superstition: The Academic Left and Its Quarrels with Science* (by P. R. Gross and N. Levitt) and an important conference sponsored by the New York Academy of Science called "The Flight from Science and Reason."

A very important episode occurred in 1996 that is referred to as the Sokal Affair. Dr. Alan Sokal, an accomplished physicist at New York University, wrote an article involving the interaction between the humanities and social studies on one hand and the objective sciences on the other. The article was submitted to an important sociology journal, *Social Text*. Indeed, the relevant issue of the journal was especially devoted to just this specific subject, the science wars. Most contributors to this issue of the journal were on the humanist-sociology "side" of the debates (the "wars"), but Dr. Sokal was clearly a well-credentialed "hard" scientist. His article, however, seemed to give much credence to important contributions that humanities could give to science. In other words, here was a well-respected scientist essentially taking the "side" of the humanist-sociologists. The article apparently, and not surprisingly, appealed to the editors, and it was published.

It became quite clear, however, that the article had not been properly reviewed prior to publication by anyone knowledgeable in physics. The treatise was a parody but not recognized as such by the editors. Indeed, it was such a well-written and magnificent parody that its publication by the journal as a serious thesis profoundly exposed deficiencies in thinking by social constructivists. To a knowledgeable physicist, the article could clearly be seen to be nonsense. The numerous subsequent debates about the article reached the level of the lay public via the common press media and caused a fair stir.

To be sure, the sociology side protested, with some justification, that the journal was not a formally peer-reviewed one. The editors trusted their credentialed contributors to be serious and ethical; thus, many humanists (but notably not all) judged the parody to be an unethical hoax. Also, in both the United States and in Europe, many academicians argued directly with some of Sokal's subsequent comments about his article. But much of the wind was taken out of the claims of the sociology side of the battles. The Sokal Affair was influential enough that it seemed to enable the science side to claim a victory in the conflict. By 1998, the science wars essentially were considered to be over.

It would be a mistake, however, to assume that the seeming end to the wars correlates with a resolution of the rift between the humanities and science. The end of the wars was mostly due to scientists assuming that, because they had won, there was no use doing any more fighting. It was deemed not worth the effort. The quiet on the war front, however, masks the continued presence of the trench that is as much a chasm as it ever was.

The relatively quiescent time during the last decade or more has not been totally without some comments about the rift. Sociobiologist E. O. Wilson published a book relating to the wars in 1998 that included a theme of "consilience" seen to be developing between the two sides. But his comments strike me as expressing a surprisingly naïve view about some of the probably intractable aspects of the problem. Many readers will recognize Stephen Jay Gould as the author of many interesting books about biologic (and evolutionary and paleontologic) subjects with humanistic relevance. His final book was published just after his death in 2002 and deals with the two cultures. Unfortunately, the book, in my opinion, is not among his more insightful works. The general tone of the work sounds to me reminiscent of the phrase "Why can't we all just get along?" à la Rodney King. In other words, the narrative implies that just the simple expression of opinions about why there shouldn't have to be irreconcilable differences between scientists and others should be sufficient, by itself, to resolve the differences. The cultural rift is deeper than that.

It would be a mistake, however, to assume that this rift means that science does not have much effect on the humanities. The science wars were mostly about the opposite—that is, what effect the humanities might have on science. It is less problematic and controversial to make judgments about the extents to which science affects the humanities and the socio-politico-economic dimensions of our world. Regardless of one's views about controversies related to the two cultures, it should be apparent that science (and related technology) stands out as a huge force in modern world development. It continues to be such, and since most scientists would probably feel they have won the science wars, the two-culture rift may have induced an overenthusiasm for science as the marvelous engine for unlimited progress. Science is a relatively definable and discrete discipline that can be examined within the complex modern civilization. Progress clearly can be discerned and described within the sphere of science. Quantitative judgments about degrees of progress, particularly technical progress, can be made. The effects of scientific progress on society at large can be examined with some probable validity. Indeed, the rift between the two cultures has enabled science to sharply stand out as the shining example of how progress is to be made. Science clearly is seen as the powerful engine for progress. Although it mostly is a one-way bridge, there is a bridge across the culture gulf from science to the humanities. And since science considers itself as having won "the wars," there may be some hubris that magnifies too much this confidence about continued progress. Since scientific progress has undoubtedly influenced the magnified optimism that can be found in the socio-politico-economic sphere, the dynamics of scientific progress are relevant to the larger societal world. It is true that some people have realized that environmental concerns tend to limit some aspects of expansive progress, but this concern is a relatively recent development and so far has had only a rather small impact on the huge optimism about unlimited progress that has developed over the last several centuries.

There is some evidence of how science has influenced political thinking throughout the twentieth century. As we have already discussed, traces of the rift can be found throughout modern world history. There was, however, a period during the first half of the twentieth century when it seemed that divisions between the humanities and science could be mended. This was during a development in philosophy that was oriented toward science called logical positivism. This movement began in Europe, mostly Vienna, but of course spread to the United States. In the latter, the ideas were sometimes referred to as logical empiricism, which emphasized the connection to science through an empiricist basis. That is, the aim was to make philosophy more valid through applying an observational bent and particularly through making philosophical statements more logically compelling. The development of the discipline of symbolic logic in the late nineteenth century facilitated this movement. Symbolic logic was applied to language, since philosophical theories had of course been expressed via language, and this was a particularly important part of this movement.

Effects on political thinking occurred via the progressive movement of the late nineteenth and early twentieth centuries. Progressive ideas initially were developed mainly in academia and not within politics per se. The ideas incorporated some aspects of the philosophy of pragmatism and its relationship to the perceived values of science. In 1887, Woodrow Wilson argued in a political journal (*Political Science Quarterly*) that there "should be a science of administration (that) shall seek to straighten the paths of government, to make its business less unbusinesslike, to strengthen and purify its organization." It was thought that governance could be made perfect by having proper governmental management, and this idea about management had a scientific flavor coming in part from the influences of logical positivism.

Needless to say, progressive ideas within politics have progressively grown until the present. The scientism instilled into political and public policy management by the progressive movement persists to this day. Macroeconomic forecasts are based on mathematical models that are attempts to make economics more scientific. There is some validity and value in this effort, but one must remain cognizant of some limitations to their predictive value. In public policy decisions, predictions based upon science-influenced thinking can sometimes border on the ludicrous. For complex socio-politico-economic issues, one can make some very short-term predictions that may have some validity, but predictions for longer terms rapidly and completely lose validity. Some reasons for this are discussed in Chapter 9. Current governmental predictions suggesting accurate forecasts of unemployment rates a year or two in the future, or predicting a specific number of jobs that will be "created" by public policies, are conveyed with an air of reliability that is not justified. Long-term budgetary or debt predictions become virtually meaningless, and yet they are promulgated to legitimize current political decisions of momentous import.

Political "science" in this context is highly limited. I will present evidence in later chapters that even formal ("true") science is limited. Since it is true science that largely has driven the optimism about progress found in contemporary political thinking, if true science is becoming limited, then surely this has significant import for politics.

Progressivism fostered the influence of science in politics, and progressivism was influenced by the philosophy of logical positivism. Later in the twentieth century, however, philosophers of science pretty much came to agree that logical positivism is not quite a valid view of science, and enthusiasm for this empiricist-based philosophy waned toward the late-middle part of the century. Most thinkers now realize that science is not as simple, not as logically reliable, and not as formally objective as we all would like. This realization partly supported the socialist-constructivist philosophies that helped foment the science wars. The war debates illustrated a "far less tidy world of science than the one depicted in textbooks. For all its technical and theoretical achievements, science is a human product and will always bear the mark of its maker" (Daniel N. Robinson). As mentioned, I will discuss further the evidence that scientific progress is more limited than most people think. There remains, however, a psychological tendency for most people, especially scientists, to "want" the scientific method to be virtually perfect. This desire still strongly influences current optimistic ideas within science, and as already mentioned, these ideas tend to affect socio-politico-economic attitudes. Therefore, in order to say some things about socio-politico-economic progress, we will now turn to examining the dynamics of scientific-technological progress.

Chapter 3
Change and S-Shaped Curves

Everyone has a general idea of what is meant by change. Some definitions would be as follows: to alter; to make different; to cause to pass from one state to another, such as to change the position, character, or appearance of a thing. Change can be in many forms. One form is a transitional or state change from one state to another. Many physical systems that exhibit change show a cyclical or oscillating change, meaning that the change goes up and down or back and forth. Many changes have elements that are irregular, chaotic, or random, but we often think of change has having some directionality. This is similar to Aristotle's idea of change having an aim or goal.

The idea of progress is a type of change with directionality. The meaning of the word includes a sense that the characteristics of something are becoming better in some way. Metaphorically, we picture progress as indicating that the characteristics of something are proceeding forward or upward over time.

As we talk about progress in coming chapters, it might be helpful to develop some ideas about how to picture progress in the "mind's eye." For this purpose, I will review some aspects of how to use diagrams or graphs as an aid for mentally picturing changes. Many readers will find this discussion overly elementary or even trite, but it may help others.

Picturing progress as going upward over time means we can represent it as a line in a two-dimensional graph with an upward axis for charting the degree (amount) of the progress and a forward ("rightward") axis for indicating the passage of time. What kinds of lines might describe most progress?

Of course, most things in the real world that we are interested in are very complex and have many components, and the characteristics of progress could not be represented as a line of simple shape. Indeed, most things could not be accurately represented in detail with only one line even if that line were a complicated one. Most changing things would require multiple complicated lines for representation because the change would be comprised of multiple, interconnected processes. But as the great physicist Newton discerned, the understanding of complex changes can often proceed quite well by beginning with a simple model to approximate things. The model can be embellished later as understanding progresses. Relatively simple lines can approximately represent most changes.

The three simplest lines that we might choose to represent progress would be a straight line angling upward as we go along the right axis, an upward line that also curves further upward, and an upward line that curves in a downward direction, thus decreasing the rate of the upward extension (Figures 1, 2, and 3). The last line, Figure 3, does not quite represent real-world progress because it begins with a very sharp, immediate increase, and generally progress does not seem to be initiated with such perfect abruption.

Line number two (curving upward) is more interesting. It is an appealing representation. Indeed, it is just this type of graph of modern progress that has insidiously infiltrated many modern minds as what we want—and, moreover, expect—our progress to have become. It is part of the aim of this book to demonstrate the impossibility of this line for representing progress.

The most well known of such simple, upward-curving lines is expressed formally as "the exponential upward curve." There are processes of change in the real world that are depicted by such a curve. For example, a nonconstrained increasing fission reaction in a nuclear device is such a process. Also, an increasingly exothermic chemical reaction is another. Note that these examples often would result in an explosion such as in a nuclear bomb or a stick of dynamite. Whether causing an explosion or something less forceful, a process in the material world following such an exponential curve results in a destructive or even catastrophic result, completely altering the process and bringing the process effectively to an end. Thus, this curve cannot be a picture of continuing, unending progress.

Before leaving the exponential upward curve, I should point out that this type of process applies not only to physical or chemical things that result in explosions but also to socio-politico-economic processes. In Germany after World War I, the exponentially increasing amount of fiat currency required to purchase a given good or service produced the disastrous inflation that catastrophically affected the country. In the United States, the accumulation of the national debt seems to be following an exponential course. The yearly additions to the debt (the budget deficits) overall clearly have an accelerating upward trend. The added interest on the debt follows a well-known exponential increase because an added amount of interest then also accumulates more interest on itself. This is mathematically defined as an exponential process. Since such a process must come to some type of catastrophic end (broadly defined), people who claim that the United States national debt is "nonsustainable" are clearly speaking the truth.

The last simple line that we might apply to progress is the upward-angling straight line. This seems to be a feasible line to at least approximate the general course of most modern progress. This line, of course, would allow unlimited progress as time marches on. We now need to think more deeply about this possibility, however.

The modern person is aware that the universe is essentially unlimited in any practical sense. Also, a number of science fiction novels, movies, and TV productions have produced some fantastic views of unlimited futures. While some of these might seem so fantastic as to be impossible, many seem to be at least slightly conceivable in the sense that they don't obviously violate any fundamental laws of physics or chemistry. In any case, these fanciful ideas can combine to produce a subtle but powerful sense that the future essentially may be almost unlimited in fantastic, but perhaps ultimately realizable, possibilities.

Most of these fantastic conceptions involve humans engaging in wondrous degrees of space travel of one kind or another. I will comment more on my views of space travel in the next chapter. Suffice it to say now that any space travel that could significantly alter mankind's state of civilization or existence is so remote in the future that it is really unforeseeable and has no practical import for current thinking. In other words, what might happen to our society and the world in any foreseeable future will not be affected by space travel.

This means that our foreseeable future is limited to this small planet we call Earth. And any person more than half aware has come to realize how small Earth really is. Many parts of the endeavors and movements of environmentally conscious people are judged by others to be extreme. Some of these criticisms are probably justified. But it is overwhelmingly obvious that the physical dimensions of societal growth are limited. Being confined to our small planet limits population growth and the utilization of partly nonrenewable resources.

If quantitative material aspects of world progress are limited, what about qualitative improvements in things other than material goods? Can we have unlimited progress in our "quality of life," governance of our civilization(s), our educational endeavors, and our ability for thinking and understanding the world? Many consider the answer to this debatable, but to me the answer is clear. Humans are clearly part of life on Earth, part of the animal kingdom. Whether your conception of humanity is mostly from a scientific-biological-evolutionary viewpoint or rather from a standpoint that is more influenced by religion, clearly humans are not gods or God. Clearly we are limited. It is true that we have a highly developed language, and we seem to be able to think with more complexity than other animals. This has caused us to very strongly differentiate ourselves sharply and qualitatively from other animals. However, I ask you to answer in a considered manner the following thought question: first, imagine a creature or being of unlimited mental abilities and powers to resolve the timeless questions of ethics and other philosophical problems—that is, a perfect creature. Of course, it is a ponderous problem to try to concretely imagine such a creature. For many, it would be like trying to picture God in detail. But whatever imagined picture you contrive, hold it in your mind. Next, picture a chimpanzee, an animal with almost all of the same genes as humans. If you examine the anatomy of a chimp brain and compare it to that of a human brain, there is much similarity. Surely the basic physiologic mechanisms—how neurons work and how they work together—are the same for both. Is a human "closer to" the chimpanzee or to the perfect being? Perhaps to help you with your answer, think of a human infant and compare that infant to a baby chimpanzee. Which is better able to function in the world? The correct answer is the chimpanzee. It is true that, shortly, the human baby will mature to far surpass the chimp in some specialized mental abilities such as imagination, introspection, and language. The point is, however, that the human, nevertheless, is inextricably a part of the animal kingdom.

For me, humans are so clearly, indubitably limited that to discuss it seems unnecessary. Since our societies are composed of humans with many limitations, our societies have limits and many of them. This means that we need to modify our straight-line graph as a depiction of feasible progress. At the upper portion of the line, we need to start to bend the line downward; the upward trend needs to start decreasing in its rate of climb.

At the beginning of the line, we should probably also make a modification. Progress is unlikely to start with an instantaneous upward slope. There almost surely would be a start-up transitional period required for "things to get up to speed." We therefore need to add an upward-curving line to the beginning of the line graph. In doing so, we then end up with a line that has an upward-bending curve at the beginning and a reversed-bending curve at the ending. This becomes essentially the very well-known sigmoid curve or S-shaped curve. The sigmoid curve is well known because it describes a great number of processes in the real world.

Sigmoid curves that are useful for some purpose often are symmetrical ones that are very much S-shaped, albeit tilted to the right. One of the best known is mathematically an essentially back-to-back exponential curve with the first portion being an exponentially increasing curve and the second component an exponentially decreasing one, with the same exponent causing the same degree of curvature for both components (Figure 4). The first part is not a perfect exponential increase because the increase is slowed more and more by the influence of the second component of the process, which is a reverse-bending curve. The middle area, the transitional area, contains what is termed the inflection point, which is where the rate of increase of the first part has been slowed enough to come to a halt and to begin to curve in the other direction.

This well-known biphasic curve is a symmetrical one that is pleasingly S-shaped. Real-world processes often are not so smooth or symmetrical. There may be very great disparities between the degrees of curvatures of the two portions (Figure 5). Some portions of the sigmoid line may be greatly stretched or greatly compressed. There may be areas in the line that have "lumpiness," an irregularity that departs from the smoothness of the simple sigmoid shape (Figure 6). Despite these departures from perfection, the sigmoid curve, considered broadly (i.e., with variations), depicts the dynamics of a very large number of processes in the world.

It is the hypothesis of this book that the changes that we regard as progress follow the sigmoid curve or variants thereof. I can't formally "prove" this assertion. I can, however, provide evidence that many processes have more limitations than are generally assumed. This will be evidence that surely many, and probably almost all, aspects of progress have at least some limits or potential limits. While there may be some components of progress that might border on exceptions to this "rule," such exceptions are highly likely to be few, minor, and perhaps illusory.

Even if one accepts the hypothesis that most change will tend to follow a sigmoid curve, there remains a big practical problem for trying to judge societal progress. It is usually very challenging to perceive where one is on the curve. At the present time, is one at an early part of the upward-bending first part of the curve or in a later portion? Is one approaching or even a bit beyond the inflection point? This is difficult because it is usually problematic to quantitate societal or political progress. Nevertheless, what one can say is that, as time proceeds, it becomes ever more likely that one is coming closer to entering into the reverse-bending portion of the curve. It becomes more and more probable that the limiting portion of the curve is "just around the corner" or perhaps already entered into. In the next few chapters, I present evidence that some important parts of technological and scientific progress, parts that almost everyone thinks are still exponentially increasing, have already entered the slowing phase or in some cases have entirely ceased to significantly progress. In like manner, it is probable that socio-politico-economic progress may be entering phases more limiting than many think.

In my claiming limits to progress, many readers may recall some of the numerous examples in history of someone predicting an ending to something and then having this prediction proved wrong by subsequent events. A very well-known physicist predicted near the end of the nineteenth century that physicists had discovered everything important about the discipline and that there was essentially nothing left of importance for physics to contribute to the world. It wasn't long until Einstein began to develop his important theories of relativity, and subsequent developments by physicists later in the twentieth century have been of much importance. I would like to note two things about such underpredictions of progress.

First, there have likely been just as many, and probably more, overpredictions of future progress, some of them bordering on the ludicrous. But such overpredictions are much harder to disprove. If such a prediction has not happened yet, perhaps the prediction just needs a bit more time to come true. The required time can extend indefinitely in the future, and thus the overprediction never becomes obviously, completely wrong. Thus, underpredictions are much more noteworthy, and the associated obvious errors are often very memorable.

Second, many of the underpredictions may have been errors in timing also. As mentioned above, judging where one is on a sigmoid curve of progress is fraught with difficulty. The fact that a physicist judged that his discipline had essentially ended and he was then proved wrong does not mean that progress in physics cannot end. Indeed, in Chapter 10, I will claim that there is evidence developing that indicates that progress in physics now may be well into the reverse-bending part of the sigmoid curve and, indeed, may be grinding toward a halt.

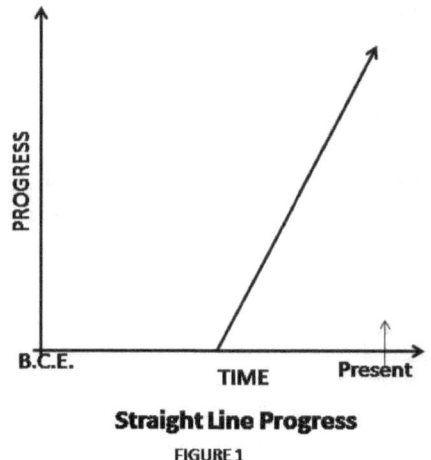

Straight Line Progress

FIGURE 1

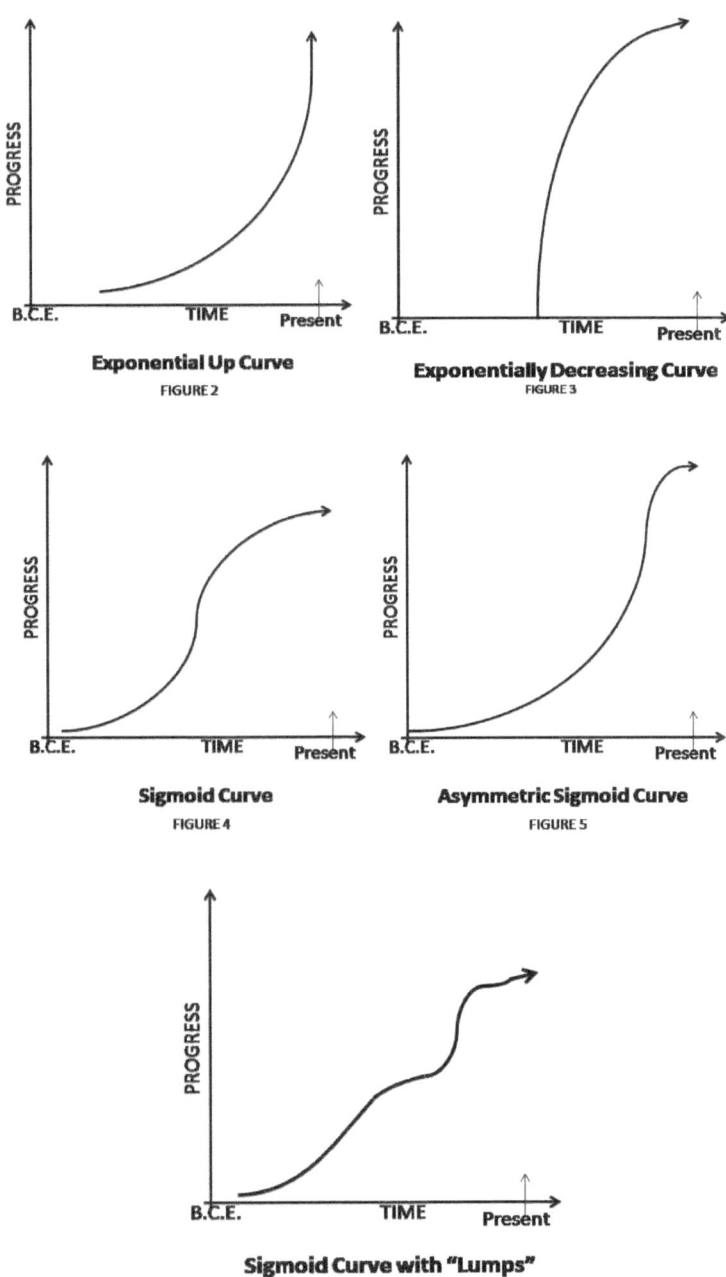

Exponential Up Curve

FIGURE 2

Exponentially Decreasing Curve

FIGURE 3

Sigmoid Curve

FIGURE 4

Asymmetric Sigmoid Curve

FIGURE 5

Sigmoid Curve with "Lumps"

FIGURE 6

23

Chapter 4

The End of the Transportation Revolution

Improvement in the transportation of people and goods is clearly one of the most important factors affecting progress in civilization throughout history. Examining transportation will provide us with one of the clearest examples of sigmoid curve dynamics, albeit a very asymmetrical one, and will show us a sharp portrayal of a limitation of progress.

A. ANCIENT AND MEDIEVAL MODES

Throughout a significantly large part of history, transportation was limited to three modes: (1) walking, (2) sitting on the back of a large animal, most commonly a horse, or in a cart pulled by such an animal, or (3) riding in a slow boat. For most of history, there was essentially no significant change in these modes. When change started, progress was so slow as to be almost imperceptible by any given individual. The beginning of the upward part of the sigmoid curve was prolonged.

Boats were either man-powered with paddles or oars or sail-driven. The directions of travel for the latter were partly at the mercy of the winds, unless oars were also available. Gradual changes in sail design and the ability to alter sail orientations afforded some gradual improvement during this period. Navigation was via celestial navigation, but without compasses or maritime clocks, navigation was limited and deeper sea voyaging was hazardous partly for this reason. The compass was developed around AD 1300.

B. RENAISSANCE

Ocean navigation was greatly improved by the development of clocks that could be shipborne. Although latitude can be determined at sea without a clock, longitude cannot be. Sextants also were important for navigation. These navigation advances fostered the transoceanic voyages that began the connection between the two world hemispheres that previously had been essentially separated and devoid of any knowledge of the existence of one by the other. This obviously began a very important part of world progress. Transportation on land, however, remained without advance during this period.

C. MODERN TIMES

Ships really started to improve with the development of the steam engine and the elimination of dependence upon fickle winds for movement and direction of movement. The upward curve in transportation progress clearly began around this time and was apparent to all. In 1807, paddle-wheel steamboats began to traverse U.S. rivers. Rivers and also canals that were built at the time were the most important means of transporting goods over the vast territories that were opening up as the United States expanded westward. Of course, these water routes had some disadvantages since many would freeze in winter and some were nonnavigable during droughts. Canals were very expensive to build and maintain.

The steam engine then was employed to develop the steam locomotive on land. The first passenger train rolled in England in 1825. In 1829, world recognition of steam engines was enhanced by a well-publicized seven-day competition in England among various locomotives. A locomotive named *Rocket* sustained a speed of twenty-eight miles per hour, the fastest land travel speed to that date.

The first well-constructed locomotive in the United States was the *John Bull*, completed in 1831. (The parts and sections of this locomotive were actually built in and shipped from England.) This began in the United States perhaps the greatest technical-economic period of progress that the world has ever known. Railroads in England were being constructed in a country that was already densely populated and commercially built up, but the vast western expanses in the United States were something very different. Those who lived some distance from rivers remained relatively isolated, and transportation of goods to these areas was difficult and expensive. In good weather, dirt roads were rough and dusty. During rainy weather, they often were muddy and even impassable. Railroads opened up these vast areas. Trains could go just about anywhere, including up and down hills and even across mountains.

By 1840, there were three thousand miles of track in the United States. By 1860, major cities and most of the larger towns were linked by thirty thousand miles of railroad track. The last three-quarters of the nineteenth century, thanks very much to railroads, was a period of absolutely astounding economic and nation-building progress.

And then came the beginning of the twentieth century with the advent of the automobile and the airplane. There is no need to detail the tremendous continued progress these wonders of transportation added to the development of the United States. It is no wonder that twentieth-century Americans developed an almost limitless optimism, engendered by a sense of certainty of a future of never-ending, always-increasing progress.

D. THE END

Alas, the era of the steam locomotive came to an end in 1960. The huge, steam-and-smoke-belching monsters, which were over a million pounds at their largest—ugly, dirty and smelly, yet wondrous, enchanting, and indispensable to the country's progress—succumbed to the diesel-electric locomotive. This was progress in that these locomotives were more fuel efficient, much easier to maintain, and of course less smoky. But there has been no significant change in locomotives since 1960 and no significant progress in railroads. Indeed, there has been some regression in the United States. (The sigmoid curves that describe so many things that change can sometimes manifest a continual reverse-bending into a downward phase, indicating regression.)

As we know, however, the nation was built with a transportation system of trains, planes, and automobiles. Hasn't there been progress with cars and airplanes since 1960? Actually, no. Most people will insist there has been, but this is a delusion fostered mainly by highly successful advertising from car companies combined with our now deeply ingrained faith in continual progress. The yearly changes in cars are mostly stylistic alterations with anything that can be considered as an improvement being only of the most minimal import. The degree to which advertisers have been successful in enticing most people to frequently buy new cars boggles my mind.

A half century ago, you would have had to punch a button down to lock a car door. Now you can lock that door and others electromechanically by pressing another type of button. This is a tiny bit of progress, but I emphasize how miniscule it is. You can now roll your window down by pushing a small button or lever. Formerly, you had to rotate a longer lever round and round. But was this really such a big chore? Multiple other minor conveniences have been added to cars, but in aggregate they have not significantly changed transportation via automobile. They certainly are not a continuance of a revolution. How important to you is cruise control? I find I don't even use it. In more crowded driving conditions, it can even be a nuisance.

Have there been significant advances in airplane travel? In 1960, there already were large passenger planes, including some jet planes. There are more of them now, but they have not significantly advanced. What about the faster Concorde plane, which could get you to Europe faster than a traditional plane? Of course, as you know, the Concorde has been discontinued. The increase in speed given by the Concorde was a minor thing, not much improvement over travel in other planes, especially when you add in airport waiting times, which would be the same for all planes. The expense of flying and maintaining the Concorde was not worth the little extra speed.

The Segway two-wheel transporter is a neat development. It was initially greeted with optimistic enthusiasm, but you don't see many of them other than at a few places like Disney World. I do not claim they are worthless. Some veterans who lost a limb in combat use Segways, and they can be a help to such people. But, overall, the addition to transportation progress is slight. Using a Segway in an area crowded with pedestrians can be a bit of a danger, although admittedly not great. In uncrowded areas, a bicycle would be faster.

E. The Future

Could the future provide some continuation of the transportation revolution? We can look at possibilities. First, we will examine changes that are now being made to make cars more efficient and greener with respect to greenhouse gas emissions. For example, a battery-powered car does not emit greenhouse gases. Many would consider this a great advance.

The first comment to make is that, in the context of this discussion, a battery-powered car is not any progress whatsoever in terms of making the actual mode or parameters of transportation different. It is still an automobile just like any other car except for the method of using energy. It is true that it will be a bit more energy efficient, but this is a change that is being driven by a need to mitigate an environmental problem. Second, the improvement in efficiency is small and limited. Electric motors are more efficient in energy use than are internal combustion engines, which waste a lot of energy through heat loss. But providing the energy stored in the battery is where the difficulty lies. This energy has to come, at present, mostly from fossil fuels, just as does the electricity that powers your home. This eliminates most of the "greenness" of battery-powered cars. As stated, it is true that electric motors are more efficient than are internal combustion engines. But part of that efficiency is compromised by the inevitable loss of energy in converting one energy form into another—in this case, burning fossil fuels and transforming the resulting energy into electricity. Then, before the electrical energy can be used in the car, there are losses in transferring that energy over long distances, and the charging of the battery entails a bit more loss.

A better example of the lack of greenness of what at first appears to many to be a very green vehicle is the proposed fuel cell car that utilizes hydrogen. The fuel cell chemically combines hydrogen with oxygen to release energy. The only waste by-product is water. What could be friendlier to the environment? But what is usually forgotten is the original energy source needed to obtain hydrogen and the many energy costs (and other problems) in getting the hydrogen into the car. Again, the original energy needed to start things comes mostly from fossil fuels. Today, 95 percent of hydrogen is produced by stripping it from natural gas. This process produces large amounts of carbon monoxide and carbon dioxide. When the hydrogen is used in the fuel cell, again there is a loss of energy in the energy-transforming step of converting the hydrogen to electricity. Also, there are practical problems of getting the hydrogen to its usage point. Hydrogen is highly flammable, and efficient storage and transportation requires the use of high-pressure containers. There would be significant monetary costs and safety concerns in getting the hydrogen into the fuel cells. Hydrogen cars offer no real progress.

A frequent image of future transportation depicts the use of small or even individual airborne vehicles for mass transportation. One could hop into such a vehicle and traverse a straight line to work without much in the way of traffic jams. This would be a significantly faster way to travel. It would, however, be costlier in energy. Lifting and translating a person in the air will require more energy than does rolling the person's vehicle along a road.

The specter of a huge number of airborne vehicles flying around a city brings with it a daunting safety problem. A little collision between two airborne vehicles is more dangerous than a comparable one between roadsters. The danger extends to those people on the ground. Perhaps you believe that having a fantastic centralized control system that is able to automatically control each air car via radio control could solve the safety problem. The passenger would need to do nothing to pilot the air car. The central control system would, of course, monitor the exact position, direction, and velocity of each vehicle continuously. Future computer systems will certainly have the capacity to continuously do the huge number of calculations needed to keep track of every vehicle almost instantaneously. Of course, the control system would run automatically with no need for error-prone human inputs.

The problem with this idea is one that was realized by NASA during the development of the space program. Early in the genesis of what would become the space program, before NASA was formed, the young U.S. Air Force (post-WWII) was performing some research experiments on the effects of acceleration on man. Some of the experiments were complicated, costly, and a bit dangerous for volunteer test subjects. For such an experiment, one wanted to be as sure as possible that the test was not going to be compromised by preventable errors or accidents. An engineer named Murphy was involved in one such test. There were twelve separate systems for monitoring and recording data from parameters reflecting physiologic effects on the subject during a large acceleration-deceleration test involving rocket sleds. Of course, many checks were done prior to instigating the sled experiment to be as sure as possible that everything functioned properly. As it turned out, it was not detected by these checks that every sensor for the twelve channels had been inadvertently hooked up in reverse so that they recorded no data. The big experiment was a total flop. Murphy could hardly believe that such a totally worthless outcome was possible. The chance of all twelve channels malfunctioning seemed almost infinitesimal.

This led to insight that later, after some variations and distortions, became known as Murphy's Law. The law since has almost always been rendered as something akin to "If something can happen, it will," or "If something bad *can* occur, then it *will* occur." This is not quite correct. The fact that something might happen does not guarantee nor necessitate that it will happen. Murphy's insight was that if there is an adverse consequence that might happen to a plan and if the consequence would be extremely adverse or costly, then one should take all feasible steps to try to prevent the adverse occurrence, *even if the adverse event is extremely unlikely.* If a mistake will entail huge cost, then large cost should be spent in trying to prevent the mistake. In other words, one should plan as if the mistake would happen, that is, pretend that it will occur. This became very important in planning to send men to the moon. The planned rocket ships were complicated and contained many systems and components. For most of these components, the chance of failure was only tiny, but if one did fail, the result could be catastrophic, both for the astronauts and for the country. NASA came to plan very safely by trying to avert a failure even if the particular failure was extremely unlikely because the consequences of most failures were so huge. One important method of doing this was by using multiple redundancies—that is, having numerous backup systems in case there was a failure in one.

But NASA eventually realized that no matter how hard they tried, perfection in safety measures cannot be attained. For example, you can't back up some things. The rocket ship has only one hull, so if heat-shielding tiles should come off the hull, there is no back-up hull. We can't make space travel perfectly safe. Of course, some major accidents have illustrated this.

If one had a huge number of airborne vehicles continually flying around a large city, there is no way that this chaos could be made safe enough by any kind of control system. There would always be a chance of a malfunction. You are not going to see such a system developed.

What about magnetic levitation high-speed railroads? Very, very expensive. Is the huge expense worth the increase in speed? Can they be made safe enough? Make your own guesses.

Let us now enter science-fantasy mode. I should note that I am not against science fiction. In fact, I grew up a big fan of space travel science fiction. But for the foreseeable future, significant space travel of a kind that would affect society will remain fiction. One of the main reasons for this assertion is that there just is no societal need for such space travel. Being able to allow some people to live on other planets is not going to solve any societal problems for those left on Earth. Such an endeavor would be unimaginably costly in many ways, and any payoffs would not be worth it.

Let's continue the fantasy with a Star Trek Transporter (STT). Recall that this is a means of transporting a person virtually instantaneously from one place to another. (The actual details of how this is done remain mysterious, although apparently the system involves changing the person into some alternate form or substance or dimension, with "quantum transportation" of the particles of the material.) For a start, a device or system such as an STT is extremely unlikely to be possible. But if it were, what would you do with it? Well, it would make it possible for you to live in Paris and work in Washington DC. You could instantly travel every day, back and forth, between the two cities. But would this be a life-changing thing for you? Is living in Paris so important? If so, perhaps you should get a job there because you are not going to get an STT. You can travel to Washington now and then by ordinary transportation.

The transportation revolution came to an end rather sharply around 1960. The reverse bending of the progress curve was highly curved (very small radius) and the sigmoid curve was quite asymmetrical, like that in Figure 5 of the last chapter. This is a poignant example of a type of progress being sharply limited. None of your birthday presents in the future will include an automobile that is significantly better in regard to transportation convenience, speed, or safety than what you have now, even if the car you have now is an old one.

Chapter 5

Medicine: Little Limits in the Bridge

In the cultural divide that tends to exist between the sciences and the humanities, medicine can be viewed as possibly being a small bridge between the two. This is because medicine has always been considered to have the quality of being both a science and an art. It combines both scientific and humanistic underpinnings and goals.

Some influence of medicine on politics can be traced back to ancient times. In Plato's *Republic,* the argument is made that rulers of the polis should have ethical regard for those ruled. An analogy is drawn using the example of the physician and the ideas of Hippocrates. The ethical physician does not put his own needs, desires, or monetary concerns in the forefront. Rather, the needs and well-being of the patient are foremost. Also, the physician is guided by scientific knowledge. Likewise, politics should be influenced by scientific knowledge. The dialogue of Plato's *Republic* is an example of an argument for science having relevance for politics, and medicine is the important part of the argument that is made in the dialogue. This is the beginning of the concept that later will be embodied in the term "political science."

In talking about modern medicine, it is more difficult to judge where we are on the curve of progress for medicine than it was for the transportation revolution. It is not so obvious that medicine has entered into the reverse-bending or slowing down portion of the curve. But it may have some hints. In any event, I can make a number of points that indicate that medicine has not always made steady and ever-increasing progress.

Medicine is not a compelling example illustrating the limits of progress. But it is of some importance in the context of this book because of the link between sciences and humanities inherent in medicine. Examples in this book that indicate that modern progress may be starting to slow are mostly from the scientific sphere. An underlying theme of the book, however, is that evidence of the slowing of the rate of progress in the scientific realm is probably relevant for the socio-political (humanistic) parts of our world also. Both sciences and humanities are endeavors of human beings, and humans have limitations. Medicine is a field wherein some of these limitations can be glimpsed.

If in some of the following comments I seem hypercritical of medicine, recall that I have a warrant for making this criticism. I am a member of the group being criticized, and I do not exempt myself from the criticism.

A. THE TIMING OF MEDICINE'S UPWARD CURVE

Compared to science in general and also to the Industrial Revolution, including the transportation revolution, the prominent upswing of the progress curve for medicine was a bit delayed. Progress didn't become really prominent until the middle or late parts of the nineteenth century.

Throughout almost all of history, including the first part of modern history, the good that doctors could do for patients was severely limited. In fact, it could be argued that some treatments, such as bloodletting with its consequent anemia and intestinal purging with its consequent dehydration, caused much of medicine to be more harmful than beneficial. It is true that a surgeon could amputate a gangrenous limb, thereby saving the patient's life, but such beneficial treatments were scarce.

In the latter part of the nineteenth century, scientists increasingly observed bacterial germs with microscopes and grew them in culture materials, thereby studying them in experimental ways. This field of bacteriology led to huge reductions in mortality by combating infectious diseases. In the beginning of the twentieth century, public health measures enabled a period of progress that marks the single greatest health advance that ever was and ever will be. This progress especially benefited from the marked improvements in the handling of sewage and the reduction in contaminants in drinking water. This was fostered by the knowledge gained by bacteriologists about the specifics underlying many important infectious diseases and their causes. In the mid-twentieth century, the development of multiple antibiotics continued this revolutionary progress in combating infectious diseases.

Anesthesia was discovered in the mid-nineteenth century, and progress in this area was a very important factor in allowing great advances in surgery. By the mid-twentieth century, most of the public generally viewed physicians as being close to gods. They were and are, of course, only human beings and not really different from other humans. Some not-so-good parts of twentieth-century medicine foreshadow the fact that this field, like other societal endeavors, is not perfect when it comes to making progress.

The lack of perfection in medicine is manifested in two ways: (1) not making progress in medicine when clearly progress could have been made, and (2) having an irrational exuberance that future progress is probably almost unlimited in regard to many medical matters. The following examples illustrate both of these aspects of the lack of perfection in the medical field.

B. No Sleep for Residents-in-Training

As I look back at my training years in medicine, there was a problem area that I thought at the time was only a problem because of my own shortcomings. As I view it now, it was more a problem of medicine in general and is an example of the amazing amount of obtuseness that the field sometimes can manifest.

Many times during some of my training (e.g., internship), I was so profoundly tired from extensive lack of sleep that my functioning was impaired, occasionally dangerously so. One episode occurred while, after having examined a patient and commencing to write important notes in the patient's chart, I blanked out. That is, I lost consciousness in the sense of having no awareness of anything and no memory from within the time period. In a way, it was like being asleep except that I continued to do things. It might be similar to the state known as sleepwalking, although it is perhaps not quite the same. Psychiatrists might call it a "fugue state," but I'm not sure. After a short while, I regained awareness and noticed that I had written extensively in the patient's official record, including orders for the patient's care. The note, however, although readable, was nonsense and gibberish. If nurses had followed some of my orders, harm to the patient may have resulted.

I recall numerous instances while I was a medical student or an intern of being involved in surgical operations. Some of the instances occurred while I was assisting in anesthesia, and this involves a lot of time being very observant of what is going on with the operation in general. Often, I would note a surgical resident holding a retractor. This can be a very boring chore because it involves pulling on the device a bit but otherwise holding still and not doing anything else for prolonged periods. Sometimes the holder cannot even see what is happening within the operative field. Residents were often so starved for sleep that I knew they could not remain fully awake. They would start to doze and naturally falter in what they were doing, occasionally starting to fall over into the operative field. The senior surgeon would then react vehemently and very often abusively, not only verbally but also physically. I've seen a number of surgical residents kicked in the posterior extremity or even hit on the head with an instrument and banished from the operating room.

What if such an impaired resident is doing something much more important for the operation than holding a retractor? Well, he or she would be able to stay awake better. But in this impaired state, certainly important errors are more likely to occur than if the resident was not so grotesquely sleep deprived. What if the resident drifted into a fugue state like mine? I am intimately aware of a number of surgical operations that have included major mishaps, occasionally fatal. Most of these were almost surely happenstance occurrences that are a reflection of the fact that humans are not perfect. But some errors are so unlikely or seemingly so stupid that one starts to wonder if impairment of the surgeon might have been a causal factor. Of course, in these individual cases, I don't know exactly why the mishap occurred, but with the frequency among residents of impairment from sleep deprivation, which I know for sure exists, it is clearly a reasonable possibility that the profound fatigue was highly causal for the mishap.

Since doctors know a lot about the functioning of human beings, clearly they know about the effects of sleep deprivation. Even nonphysicians know about this. How can medicine abide having trainees take care of patients while severely impaired on account of a lack of sleep? The answer has always been that a trainee learns much more if a hundred hours or so are worked per week on the job, including extended periods with no sleep. Part of the idea behind this answer is that, with a seriously ill patient in the hospital who requires almost continual care, if a resident is not present to be the main supervisor of care during all of that time, then the learning experience is greatly compromised. Perhaps the learning is a little bit compromised. But how effective is the learning if the learner cannot stay awake? Any little extra bit of ineffective learning that occurs in such a circumstance is much overshadowed by the negative effect of the danger to patients.

When I was a senior in medical school, I recall an incident that occurred at about one o'clock in the morning. I was in the radiology department examining some radiographs (X-rays). A man I knew who was a year ahead of me in training, and at this time doing his internship in internal medicine, was also there examining radiographs taken of some of his patients. I noticed that he was silently crying. I asked what was wrong. He said he was so continuously, horribly tired from lack of sleep that he didn't know how he was going to "make it." He clearly was devastated. The severity of his emotion has caused the incident to be indelible in my memory.

A small reduction in this problem has occurred with a few modest restrictions having been placed on the previously unlimited working hours expected for residents. But this change did not come from within medicine. It resulted from legal actions taken by some people, usually injured patients or dead patients' relatives, who unfortunately became too intimately aware of the problem.

This is an example of the type of thing that, over the decades, has made the following clear to me. Physicians are still generally considered to be very smart. It is true that one has to have good grades in college to enter medical school. It is also true that doctors know a great deal about diseases and are generally good at treating patients with the diseases. But when it comes to other areas of functioning, including the numerous things that fall into the category of common sense, doctors are certainly no brighter than anyone else.

C. SMOKING AND CANCER

About a decade ago, I had the opportunity to examine in detail the histologic (microscopic) slides prepared from the cancer that eventually killed President Ulysses S. Grant. The slides are remarkable in that they date from the very earliest part of the beginning of the examination of biopsies of tumors under the microscope for treatment purposes (Grant's tumor biopsy was done in 1885). The purpose of my examination was to write a detailed modern report on the slides for the archives of the National Museum of Health and Medicine, where the slides are maintained.

In the course of this examination, I read a few things about the circumstances surrounding the diagnosis of the tumor and the treatment of President Grant. As is well known, Grant was a heavy drinker and a very frequent cigar smoker. Grant developed cancer of the throat near the tonsils. His physicians were absolutely certain that the cigar smoking was a causal factor for his cancer, and they insisted that he stop smoking. Of course, by then it was too late to do any good.

When I was in medical school, I recall patients on the ward where head and neck cancer patients were treated. I remember how many were heavy smokers, as well as heavy drinkers or alcoholics. My teachers were well aware of the strong causal link between smoking and most of these cancers. Of course, the great importance of this factor for most lung cancer patients was also well known. The question I asked myself then—but alas, didn't vocalize much to anyone else—was, why isn't something being done to reduce the rate of smoking? I just assumed then that nothing could be done.

I now know how certain Grant's doctors were of the causal effect of smoking for his cancer, and this emphasizes just how long doctors have known this important fact with all reasonable certainty. The fact that some people can smoke all their adult lives and still be well in their nineties is not evidence against this fact; as will be discussed in the next chapter, cancer is caused by multiple factors that accumulate in a mostly random manner. The heavy smoker living in his or her nineties is just very lucky. And yet, for so many decades, nothing significant was done by the medical community to try to reduce smoking levels. In retrospect, many would argue that it would have been difficult to do anything significant for a number of reasons, particularly because of the corporate power of cigarette producers. This is no excuse. This was a failure of medicine.

D.   BREAST CANCER STUPIDITY

In the early part of the twentieth century, the famous surgeon William Halstead developed the radical mastectomy as a treatment for breast cancer. This became the accepted treatment virtually everywhere. Its acceptance was legitimate because, for the majority of patients that Halstead treated, this was the only effective treatment available. Most of the patients' conditions had not come to a doctor's attention until the tumor was quite large, often huge. Radical mastectomy was the only choice.

Not surprisingly, the operation had some significant adverse side effects. It required removing huge amounts of tissue, including all the muscles in the upper part of the chest on the affected side. These muscles controlled part of arm movement, and thus arm movement was compromised. The surgical effort was aimed at thoroughly removing all traces of lymphatic nodes and channels in a large anatomic region to try to prevent the spread of the tumor. Removing all of these lymphatics meant that often the lymphatic drainage from the arm was compromised enough that the arm became hugely and permanently swollen. This was very uncomfortable. Also, occasionally this would lead to a malignancy of the lymphatic channels in the arm. Of course, the operation was very disfiguring. These adverse effects, however, were judged worth it because otherwise the patient would die from the breast cancer. Unfortunately, most patients died from the cancer anyway as it had already spread too far before the operation. But for the few survivors, the operation was worthwhile.

Fifty to seventy years later, things had changed significantly regarding when patients with breast cancer were first seen by a physician. At that point, many such patients presented with quite small tumors. Yet the standard treatment, radical mastectomy, remained the same. It was judged by the surgical community to be the gold standard treatment, and a god of surgery had developed it. One does not question a god's work.

When I was a resident-in-training for surgical pathology, I examined quite a few radical mastectomy specimens. They usually contained only a small tumor in the breast, sometimes just a tiny one. The mastectomy specimens were thoroughly dissected to look for evidence of tumor outside the breast. Sometimes there were moderate-sized metastatic deposits of the cancer in the lymph nodes of the armpit. Sometimes the deposits were found only under the microscope. And sometimes there were no deposits. But in all of these cases, I was impressed that never did I find any evidence of any tumor within, between, or around the massive amounts of muscle and associated tissue that had been removed from the upper chest. The argument of the surgeons was that these tissues needed to be removed to be sure all the lymphatic channels had been removed, but there were never any lymph nodes in these locations. The tiny, microscopic channels that were present somewhere within these tissues and that led to the lymph nodes in the armpit never had tumor in them; the tumor cells did not stop and grow in these conduits. Much experimental work had been done that indicated that tumor cells did not become stuck in these channels, but rather only in the nodes. Was it really necessary to remove so much tissue when treating a small tumor?

Good evidence was accumulating that it was not always necessary to do so, nor was it even advisable. Cures could be obtained with much lesser operations. Almost all of the surgical community, however, was strongly resistant to any change for the radical mastectomy. Two brothers, one a surgeon and one a pathologist, gradually collected large amounts of very good evidence that the surgical procedure could be safely modified (lessened) for the benefit of patients. The surgeon, Dr. Bernard Fisher, tried to communicate this to his surgical colleagues by extensively lecturing and writing about it. But this was of no avail for many, many years. Moreover, surgical colleagues often treated Dr. Fisher, who was attempting to make progress, very harshly and even cruelly.

One colleague of mine had attended a large conference devoted to this subject at a major university medical center. The chairman of the surgical department at the center was so vehemently cruel in his abusive criticism of the lecturing surgeon in public before a plenary audience that my colleague was flabbergasted.

Gradually, the evidence won out because it became overwhelming. But the merited changes were delayed decades past the time when they should have been instigated. It is true that changing standard and proven beneficial treatments should not be done without careful circumspection and without good reasons. But in this case, the degree of resistance to progress was not warranted and was harmful.

E. *Wishful Thinking about Infections*

In the late 1960s, the U.S. Public Health Surgeon General examined the progress made in treating infectious diseases and concluded that very soon infectious diseases would no longer be any significant health problem. Shortly, we would have essentially defeated them. He even testified before Congress and gave this opinion. Needless to say, this was a poor judgment. Clearly this has not happened, and it won't. This is surely an example of irrational exuberance regarding estimates of the powers of medicine for making progress.

As even the public now well knows, many infectious agents have the ability to mutate and acquire resistance to antibiotics or other chemical treatments. Many agents have the characteristics to allow for epidemic rates of spread. Increased rates of travel among the world's inhabitants foster the spread of many infectious diseases that were formerly more limited in their geographic distribution. New infectious agents can become manifest, as exemplified by AIDS. In regard to AIDS, one might think that modern medicine could rather easily develop a preventive vaccine since we have done that for many other infectious diseases. Over the last quarter century, however, we have not been able to do it for AIDS. Infectious diseases will not be totally eradicated. Indeed, some have become more problematic with time. Clearly, we are not seeing unlimited progress.

F. *No Flow, No Go*

As mentioned above, the period of the greatest progress in improving the health of citizens in the Western world involved public health measures that improved sewage management, as well as provided clean water. This greatly reduced deaths caused by sewage-mediated, waterborne infectious diseases. It is in this context that I discuss the following contemporary fiasco in sewage management. Although this mistake apparently did not result in a serious increase in such infections, it certainly could have. In any case, the mistake serves as an example of a retrogressive action with the potential to adversely affect huge numbers of people. I am referring to the push to develop and spread the use of low-flow toilets. Low-flow toilets have been engineered to use less water for flushing than do conventional commodes. The rationale for this was, of course, to conserve water.

The problem with this effort was that the new toilets did not flush as cleanly as the ones using larger amounts of water. The new toilets almost flushed adequately, but they used a borderline amount of water that meant that sometimes the flush would clearly not be clean.

When used in personal homes, the problem was not a big one because users would just flush the toilet twice. But this meant that the water-saving purpose of the new toilets—the only reason for developing such toilets—was much compromised. The bigger problem arose from placing the toilets in public facilities. Users in this context seldom bothered to flush the toilets twice.

The residual fecal waste in such toilets provided the type of contamination that had formerly plagued civilization prior to modern sewage-waste handling. Only a small amount of such waste is required to provide huge numbers of bacteria. Also, the bacteria can multiply rapidly. Bacteria causing the types of diseases spread by this route have evolved to make very effective use of just such a means of spread provided by contaminated toilet water. It has been experimentally shown that flushing a toilet produces microparticles of water that are flung upward and out from the toilet. This of course can contaminate a toilet user.

Toilets have recently been installed in many public facilities that have an automatic flush function. A sensor detects when a user departs the toilet seat. This certainly sounds like a good idea. The problem is that sometimes movement activates the sensor while the user is still on the toilet seat.

Does this information make you a bit more reluctant to use public toilets? It should.

I present one last toilet note, the development of what I call girly toilets. These are toilets that are chic, svelte, and pleasing to the eye. They are built low to the floor. This improves the appearance, but think for a moment. To have adequate water in the bowl for the purpose, a low toilet seat means that the water surface is not very far from the toilet seat. This is all right for women. But men have a different anatomy in their nether bifurcation. One does not want to have this anatomy dipped in toilet water. I occasionally have encountered girly toilets installed in public men's rooms.

Wouldn't you classify these innovations as something less than progress? Modern toilet innovations clearly are not an area of modern progress. Where were comments from the medical community about this?

G.   WAR ON CANCER

In 1971, President Nixon announced a government-supported and heavily funded effort to eliminate or cure cancer. Although he did not use the term in the announcement, this prolonged and currently continuing effort became known as the war on cancer. All would agree that this sounds like a very worthwhile effort. Note, however, that the aim was not to make some progress in treating cancer, but to cure it, to conquer it, to banish it from the human condition. This is unrealistic hubris, and the evidence from the last thirty-eight years of the war supports my assertion.

Yes, there has been some progress in treating cancer over this period. Most of this progress, however, has come from efforts different from the research efforts funded from the many billions of dollars spent by the launch of this governmentally supported mission. The mission was to support basic research directed at really trying to understand the causes of cancer on the most fundamental and detailed biologic level possible. Conducting the most cutting-edge research was viewed as the only way of finding the *cure*. This seems a logical assertion, and it indeed probably was a very reasonable one. The profound problem underlying this idea, however, is the fact that Mother Nature sometimes does not want to cooperate with us. The reasons underlying this problem are multiple. Some I will briefly address here, and these are mostly ones now well known to the biological medical community. Two other reasons, however, are more profound and important, and these two hardly are appreciated or even known by most in the medical community. I address these two reasons in Chapters 6 and 9.

First, let us be clear about the sources of most of the progress that has been obtained over the last (almost) four decades. The main categories are: (1) preventive measures; (2) early detection screening measures; (3) serendipitous (fortuitous) advances made by trial-and-error guesswork and then by conducting multiple large clinical trials that try different combinations and variations of therapies already developed; and (4) tiny, multiple advances in the three classic therapeutic modalities of surgery, radiotherapy, standard chemotherapy (i.e., not directed by "targeting" molecular biologic factors for each individual tumor), with minor but cumulative steps added to the effectiveness of these standard therapies by improving the specific diagnostic classifications of cancers within my field of surgical pathology. Note that none of these four categories of progress resulted from the basic research directions launched by the war on cancer. More important for our discussion, note also that most of the advances obtainable by these four areas of improvement have probably already been obtained. In other words, we have entered into the slowing or reverse-bending parts of the progress curves for these areas. This is the portion of the progress curve that shows ever-diminishing returns for a given amount of effort. Of course, some people would argue that we have not entered into such a region of the curve, but one purpose of this book is to try to enlighten such people.

An example of a preventive factor that has been important is smoking-cessation efforts. In 1971, 54 percent of men in the United States were smokers; today, it is about 21 percent. This is a very important progress. (The numbers are not so good for women.) For women, the realization that estrogen hormone replacement tended to promote the development of some cancers has resulted in a more restricted and judicious use of these hormones, and this has prevented some cancers that would have otherwise been promoted. Increased knowledge about the cancer-promoting effects of some chemicals has allowed some prevention by mitigating the exposure to some of these agents. The important causal role that the human papilloma viruses have for some cancers, particularly cervical cancer, has enabled a reduction in the occurrence rates of these cancers.

There are several important examples of cancer mortality reduction through earlier detection of the cancers by screening methods. Mammography for breast cancer is one. Colonoscopy for detecting colon cancer is an important one. Conducting PAP smears to detect cervical cancer has been a very effective measure. PSA screening for prostate cancer has been of some importance, but it has been less effective in reducing death rates.

Regarding effective therapies discovered through the process of trial-and-error serendipity, there are important examples for a few childhood cancers. Childhood leukemia is an outstanding example. The cure rate has gone from dismal, around 5 percent, to superlative, greater than 90 percent. Significant advancement has also been made for brain tumors in children. These advances were made not through any basic research breakthroughs in understanding, but rather through plodding, "brute force" work devoted to trying new combinations, doses, sequence changes, and timing changes of drugs already developed. While these great improvements have been extraordinarily gratifying for the affected children and their parents, the same type of progress has not been forthcoming for the much more common adult cancers. (There are a few rare exceptions, such as treatment for testicular seminoma.) The reason for this difference is that the childhood cancers are biologically much simpler in their causal factors. That is, the development of these cancers is often predominantly because of one causal factor, a specific and usually congenital genetic mutation or chromosomal defect. Adult cancers are almost always multifactorial in causation, and this leads to a much more daunting problem for seeking a cure (see below).

While these types of progress indeed have been significant, the overall picture for cancer is less impressive. The instances of significant progress for specific cancers have of course received thorough publicity, and these hopeful results tend to obscure the larger picture. That picture includes many areas that are not only less hopeful but dismal. Some important cancers are increasing in their occurrence rates. Since for many of these cancers the death rates have not significantly decreased, the overall population death rates for them have increased. Lung cancer death rates rose from 43 to 53 per 100,000 persons in the three decades following 1975. This is *in spite of* the very beneficial effect of a large decrease in smoking among men. The death rate from malignant melanoma has also increased. For cancer of the liver and bile ducts, the death rate has doubled. The high death rate for pancreatic cancer has not improved. These are all cancers with frequent occurrence in the population.

Overall, the progress in fighting cancer has been much more limited than most people suppose. In 1975, the U.S. death rate due to cancer was 199 per 100,000 persons in the population. In 2005, it was 184 per 100,000, a decrease of only 7.7 percent over thirty years of the war on cancer. This becomes less impressive when compared to a period from before the war began. Between 1950 and 1967, the death rate from cancer among women fell from 120 to 109 per 100,000. This was a larger decrease (9.2 percent) over about half the time period than during the thirty-year war period. The decrease during this earlier period was due to measures that had nothing to do with the molecular biologic research focus that underlies the optimism that started the now four-decade-long war.

Why has the war not been more effective? One reason has been related to the fact that much of the research efforts have involved experiments on mice. There are some almost intractable problems in relating such research to humans. Some of the causes of these problems are now well understood among researchers. I believe, however, that these problems are compounded a bit by the profound factors that I discuss in Chapters 6 and 9 and that are not well understood by most researchers.

An initial glimpse of the problems discussed in these later chapters can be seen in the following comments. Among the general public, there is a perception that a given cancer must have a cause, that is, a single cause. This is not so. For almost all cancers, the causal chain consists of multiple causes, including at least more than half a dozen individual cumulative steps. The steps are mostly independent from one another, meaning that they occur at different, unrelated time intervals and not necessarily in a given sequence. More important, most are random in regard to if, when, and where in the body they occur.

Most of the steps are mutational effects on DNA, which may be inborn or caused by radiation effects, chemical effects, or unknown causes. Radiation effects can result from radiation generated by man, such as therapeutic X-rays, diagnostic CT scans, nuclear medicine therapies, or nuclear weapons or nuclear power side effects, although the latter are actually much more rare than most people suppose. Radiation effects that result from background radiation come from radioactive elements in the earth and from cosmic rays.

When ionizing radiation, from whatever source, enters the body, the particular cell or cells that it affects are mostly random in location. As mentioned, most of the other steps in the causal chain of cancer are also random. Their timing of occurrence and location of occurrence are unpredictable. This means that the development of a given cancer in a given individual is largely random. Thus, when an individual asks his doctor why the cancer developed, the correct answer in most instances is "bad luck." I certainly do not mean to be flippant about this serious point. It would be insensitive to say directly to a patient that that his or her cancer was caused simply by bad luck. This is, however, the truth of the matter.

With this fact in mind, perhaps the reader can begin to sense the magnitude of the challenge faced by those who aim to rid the world of cancer. In the next chapter and also in Chapter 9, we will examine more deeply some of the reasons that we lack control over the ability to really win the war against cancer. We will perceive some limits that Mother Nature has placed in the world for us.

Chapter 6

The Limits of DNA

Most readers will be aware of the excitement surrounding the sequencing of the entire human genome that was completed near the end of the last decade. What a great advance to begin the new millennium. It seems, however, that hardly anyone is aware of two stumbling blocks that I perceive that will greatly inhibit the rate of progress in utilizing this accomplishment. The two fundamental factors are (1) the limits of the digital information coding of DNA for controlling most cellular biochemical dynamics and (2) the influence of deterministic chaos in cellular dynamics. (The second factor will be discussed in Chapter 9.)

A. Our Heritage of a Clockwork Universe

Failure to appreciate these factors results in part from the profound impact of classical (Newtonian) physics on the nature of the world as viewed by Western scientists and other thinkers. For several centuries, there has been a widespread certainty that the world we live in obeys Newton's laws of motion. In doing so, the world becomes highly predictable and also controllable. There is a mechanistic cause and effect underlying all change. The late-eighteenth-century mathematician P. S. de Laplace emphasized this by proclaiming that if enough data were available regarding the positions and velocities of the elements of matter at a given time, then all future events could be explicitly calculated and predicted. Although there are obvious practical problems in collecting all the requisite data, the philosophy underlying this viewpoint has pervaded science in a profound way. Subsequent developments in relativity theory and quantum mechanics have not much changed this. The Heisenberg uncertainty principle of quantum mechanics states that we cannot know the exact position and velocity of a subatomic particle at a given time. This often is interpreted as destroying determinism, but it actually doesn't quite do that. The principle indicates the impossibility of collecting all the requisite data, but on a basic or philosophical level determinism might still exist. In particular, the uncertainty principle did not affect the supra-atomic (macroscopic) world in which we all live, and in this world Newton's deterministic laws still rule. Some systems have so many elements that stochastic (probabilistic, statistical) methods must be used for practical purposes, but very useful analysis is still possible.

Some dynamic processes, such as turbulence in fluids, are represented by nonlinear equations that are not formally solvable, and up until half a century ago, these processes threatened to remain intractable problems for detailed deterministic analysis. Then, however, along came the digital computer. Computer assistance can allow the practical near-solution of many nonlinear differential equations by iterative (repeated) approximate calculations. With enough repetitions, these approximated calculations can achieve a high accuracy. It then seemed that there was no stopping scientists, and their rate of progress in calculating and figuring things out was tacitly assumed to be exponentially increasing and seemed almost unlimited. Biology remained a very complicated challenge at many levels, however. But then along came DNA.

B. THE DELIGHTFUL DIGITAL DETERMINISM OF DNA

Upon learning the molecular structure of DNA, almost everyone can readily appreciate that this "secret of life" is something very special indeed. It is an almost intuitive understanding. The DNA molecule includes four different compounds that chemically have a basic pH, and for this reason they are referred to as bases. These four bases can be thought of as being the same thing as letters, and thus they can carry information as letters do when formed into words. The sequence of bases in the DNA molecule thus is able to code (carry, stand for) information, just as words code information. There is an adjacent additional sequence of bases, the complementary strand, which also codes the same information, albeit in a reverse or opposite sense. The molecule thus can split into two parts, and this process can use one of the strands to pass the information on to another process or to a daughter cell. The complementary strand also serves as an error-checking mechanism in case one of the bases should accidentally be replaced with another, incorrect base. If this happens, the DNA has an associated mechanism for repairing the error.

The four-based coding and complementary structure of the DNA double (i.e., two-strand) helix are so elegantly simple and yet so obviously amazingly powerful, it almost makes one want to shout, "Why didn't we figure this out long ago? It so obviously has to be this way. How else could it be?" The rapturous appeal of this structure arises partly because it is intuitively clear how this meshes with our understanding of the deterministic nature of our world. The coding in the DNA sequences provides an obvious method for tight and almost error-free control of the processes of life. Therefore, if we figure out all of the control codes and the control processes, we can—dare we say it?—figure out all of life! No wonder the sequencing of the genome has caused dancing in the streets.

Although almost everyone can understand the general functioning of DNA coding, few understand it in its most basic and fundamental essence. Such profound understanding is not necessary for most purposes. For our purpose of understanding the limits of DNA, however, such understanding is important. We will now embark on an explication that is a bit difficult, but it may be rewarding.

C. Why Digital Is "Cool"

The power of DNA coding derives from the fact that it is a digital information carrier, and the power derives solely from that fact. This is remarkable because the world in general does not utilize digital information mechanisms, but rather such mechanisms are analog. DNA is a rare exception. (The difference between analog and digital information will be addressed shortly.)

Everyone knows that modern computers are digital and that such computers are very important. Also, many other devices, such as telephones, TVs, and music media, have become digital, and generally digital is considered the best. But why is digital the best? Why is digital "cool"?

It is surprising how few people, including scientists, fully understand the nature and fundamental advantage of digital information. This even seemingly includes some who actually do technical or engineering work in fields involved in information processing. Books on information theory often do not provide any clearly defined and cogent description of, or definition of, the most basic aspects of digital information and its advantages. It might be thought that this is because the authors assume that the reader already knows such basic details. Yet, the same authors may include some definitions or brief notations about some words or concepts that are so simple and widely known that most elementary school children have learned them. This lack of emphasis on the basic advantage of digital information is puzzling.

Information is the antithesis of uncertainty. Information combats, decreases, and relieves uncertainty, and thus it can be very useful in a mostly uncertain world. For these purposes, information is processed and stored or transmitted, received, and stored by others. Particularly while being transmitted, but also during processing, information is subject to numerous interfering, distorting, and degrading effects (atmospheric, electrical, mechanical, thermal, quantum, etc.), which we will subsume under the word "noise." Noise is a big problem for trying to maintain the integrity of information. Engineers refer to the signal-to-noise ratio (S/N), and the bigger it is, the better it is for preserving information. The higher the S/N, the lower is the loss of information.

There are two forms in which information can exist (i.e., be encoded within)—analog and digital. (Mathematical topological information possibly is a third form or means.) These two forms are mathematically related to, or analogous to (i.e., can be depicted by), graphical plots of either continuous lines, including curves, or plots of discrete points. Digital information is in a discrete form—that is, depicted by a plot of points. It is sometimes said that digital information is represented by numbers, but this shows a lack of complete understanding. Digital representation (encoding) is made by means of special numbers, the *integers*. No fractions, whether expressed as decimal numbers or otherwise, are allowed. When a decimal fraction is represented and used in a digital computer, where only integers are used, it is represented in "floating point notation" as an integer multiplied by base 10 (an integer) raised to an integer power. The computer utilizes only integers for processing; the digital nature of the processing demands this. When letters are entered into a computer via a keyboard, the letters are converted into a representation using integers.

Analog information is exemplified by measurements wherein the measuring instrument has a continuous scale, such as a voltmeter that has a mechanical pointer that moves to any place on a visible continuous scale. When a person steps on a mechanical weight scale, the pointer can come to rest anywhere along the continuous pound indicator scale. A mercury thermometer and a fluid barometer are analog devices. If one drew a graph of the possible measurements, these devices would have a readout along a continuous line. The points in a continuous analog line include an infinite number of decimal fractions.

Why is this important? The importance is related to the S/N ratio. Unless the ratio is unusually small (i.e., the noise is overwhelmingly large), digital information is essentially impervious to degradation from noise. Analog information is always altered by noise, even if the noise is very small. The advantage of digital information can be understood from an example such as a pulse-code-modulated (encoded) radio signal transmission. If the transmitted signal is encoded into discrete (countable) pulses, usually square wave pulses, the only job the receiver has to do is determine whether or not a pulse is present at any instant of time. If the pulse has been altered by noise, with its amplitude, for example, having been increased or decreased by 10 percent, or if the corners of the pulse have been rounded or the pulse shape otherwise altered, this is of no consequence. The altered pulse will be detected by the receiver as being present and will thus be counted by the receiver. The count is indicated and perhaps stored by the receiver as an integer, for example, integer 1. The count is the same regardless of whether or how the pulse has been degraded by noise. Thus, the transmitted information remains highly reliable (i.e., "perfect").

An example of the effectiveness of a type of pulse-code-modulation can be found in the famous Morse code. The dots and dashes of this code were in the length or time ratio of 1 to 3. Although the code was a relatively slow means of information transfer, its digital nature made it highly effective in the days when telegraphic or radio transmissions were subjected to large amounts of noise and signal strengths were often very small. Thus, the S/N ratios were often only marginal for any reliable information transfer. In Morse coding, the receiver, usually a human ear and brain, had only to make two determinations: (1) whether a signal (a pulse) is present or not and (2) whether the signal length is closer to 1 or 3 units. Both of these discriminations can readily be made in the face of marked changes in signal strength, shape, or alterations in signal frequency components as well as in the presence of other prominent random noise influences.

In most computer applications, the number of processing steps is incredibly large. If occasional errors from noise were to occur, they would add up to overwhelmingly huge errors when the number of processing steps was very large. The only way computers are able to reliably function is that the information being processed remains essentially perfect. Digital encoding enables such perfection.

Although biological evolution requires that occasional errors occur in DNA, in the shorter term—the term in which we all live—it is obviously critical that the information carried by DNA be highly stable and reliably reproducible when received and recorded (i.e., when copied and then passed on during cell division and the formation of new daughter cells). This information transmission is accomplished by the quaternary code of A, C, G, T (which can be equivalently represented by the four integers 1, 2, 3, 4 or, alternatively, 0, 1, 2, 3). These are the first letters of the four bases that comprise the information part of the DNA strands. Chemical compounds different from, or "between," these four are not allowed, just as decimal numbers between the integers are not allowed in coding digital information.

The complementarity, or doubled state, of the DNA double helix enhances stability. If an occasional error (noise) should creep into the sequence of the DNA bases, complementarity serves as the starting point for a repair mechanism that corrects the error. In this regard, the single-stranded RNA molecules that serve as information carriers in many viruses have much less stability; this is why such viruses—for example, flu viruses—are very frequently mutated. This point concerning the stability of digital information is potentially confusing. Over what period of time must the information remain perfectly stable? How stable must stable be? If an information system has multiple steps and only one of these steps, such as a processing step, utilizes digital information and the other steps are analog processes, stability is required only for the digital processing step. When multiple steps of transmission, receipt, recordation, and storage are required—and this will be true for most systems using digital information—long periods of virtually perfect stability are required.

DNA is and remains essentially perfect for its purposes as an information carrier. Processing and computations on the basis of such information should also be capable of being perfect. Dynamics (changes) based upon such information should be perfectly predictable. Because DNA is the initial controller of biologic cell dynamics, we should eventually be able to compute and predict cellular functions virtually perfectly. This is immensely appealing to our sense of accurately computable deterministics, which is based on the bedrock of centuries of science and mathematics. No wonder molecular biologists and physicians heavily involved with DNA pursuits are flying high!

D. The Deflation of DNA Digital Determinism

Unfortunately, the digital power of DNA is mostly left upon the doorsteps of cellular transcription and translation. These are the initial steps within the cell that transform the information carried by DNA into forms that are used in cellular biochemical processes. For example, the step of translation refers to the transmission of the DNA code to the little manufacturing sites called ribosomes that construct proteins. The amino acids that make up proteins are aligned in a sequence that mirrors the digital information of DNA. This is called the primary structure of the proteins. There are, however, overall shapes to the protein molecule, called the secondary and tertiary structures. While these shapes are related to the underlying primary structure, they are not a completely rigidly deterministic reflection of it. In other words, some wiggle room has started to appear. This wiggle room means that the information carried by the protein has started to lose its digital determinism. It has begun to take on characteristics of analog information.

Proteins are immensely important for the cellular processes. Some proteins make up part of the structural framework of the cells. Other proteins are enzymes, which are hugely important in controlling cellular biochemical dynamics. These biochemical dynamics involve information that is highly analog in character. The information storage perfection of DNA is no longer utilized or required for these biochemical purposes.

It has been argued that some biochemical regulation and control circuits have digital features. Most such arguments are faulty. For example, there are control mechanisms that utilize what is called RNA interference. RNA has digital information, although it is not highly stable as is DNA information. RNA interference utilizes RNA fragments that are about two dozen bases in length, contrasted with the many millions in DNA molecules. Does the sequence of these two dozen bases constitute digital information? Well, yes, but it has been degraded from genomic information in a way analogous to chopping up a book into individual phrases or words and intermixing them. The words and phrases represent some information, but most of the information contained in the sentences and paragraphs of the book has been lost.

Epigenetic processes might be viewed as having a digital character. Epigenetic processes are control influences that can be passed on to daughter cells, but they are not genetic, meaning they are not based on the transmission of DNA base sequence information. Most of these influences involve methylation (the addition of a methyl molecule) to various sites of DNA molecules. These methylations alter the DNA molecular form in subtle ways that can influence biochemical processes that the DNA molecules are involved in. The process of methylation is a discrete one; that is, specific, individual chemical sites are involved. Moreover, the specific sites that have been methylated can be determined in the laboratory. The sites can then be counted in a binary fashion (i.e., methylated or not, 1 or 0), and the methylations are at least somewhat stable, albeit about four orders of magnitude less so than is DNA. It is extremely doubtful, however, that the cell counts and records these sites in this digital fashion. A mechanism for doing so does not seem to exist and, more important, does not seem necessary or even advantageous for cellular purposes. Analog processing of the information (embodied in biochemical processes) related to methylation is just fine for the use of the information in the cellular dynamics that are influenced by the information.

It should be pointed out that information processing in complex systems with multiple processing steps can involve both digital and analog steps. When this happens, the overall system becomes an analog one. That is, even though a digital step may be impervious to noise, the fact that other steps in the processing chain are analog, and thus degradable by noise, means that the overall processing becomes subject to noise degradation—that is, it becomes analog.

It may seem to the reader strange to be using the word "information" in respect to biochemical processes. This is because most people tend to think of information in a limited way. We think of it as mainly carried by spoken or written language. But this is a limited view of information. Information is critical in many other settings, including the basic processes of life.

In a lecture to a medical audience, I presented some of these ideas about information control in cellular processes. A biochemist friend of mine in the audience commented that biochemical processes do not really involve information mechanisms as I was asserting. He stated that using the word "information" in this context was "only a metaphor." Well, no, actually it is not just a metaphor. Coming from a highly educated scientist, this lack of appreciation for the fundamental import of information control surprised me at the time. In retrospect, however, it no longer surprises me because I now know the almost ubiquitous extent of such lack of complete understanding.

There are biochemical cellular processes that can be viewed as equivalent to a threshold on-off (i.e., binary digital) switch and that are probably used in some biochemical cellular control and regulating circuits. This has been used to tacitly imply a digital information component to the control circuit. There are, however, two kinds of on-off switches: (1) momentary pulse switches (e.g., for your car horn) and (2) bistable "state change" switches or "latching" switches (e.g., ordinary household light switches). Digital information processing requires a bistable, state change switch. The biologic (biochemical) switches are momentary switches; they are "on" only as long as the input signal stays on. Momentary switches could be used to transmit a digital count, but only if the pulse were counted and recorded, or received and read, by some bistable, state change mechanism. Highly bistable mechanisms generally are not present in cellular control circuits and networks. It is true that feedback (autoregulatory) controls in some networks can effect a signal "locking" that approaches bistability, but this offers only a very feeble degree of "digitality" that surely is overwhelmed by the analog processes in the cell. Recall that having any analog steps means that the overall system is analog. Any stability of autoregulatory locking is dependent upon unceasing, uninterrupted, continuous signaling in the feedback loop of the control circuit (see Chapter 12). This perforce confers a weak point regarding stability.

The lack of understanding that receiver-recorder mechanisms, which are necessary for digital information transfer, are not present in most biological systems causes a widespread misperception that DNA digital control is more pervasive than it really is. This is a very important misperception in that it contributes a great deal to the over optimism about the extent of what can be accomplished with the knowledge from the sequencing of the human genome. Trying to control or eliminate cancers will be a much harder task than most people think.

As I have been writing this, a large snowstorm has occurred outside my window. This has brought to mind an analogy that may help in understanding the meaning of what I have focused on in this chapter. It is a rather loose analogy, but it may serve to indicate the significance of the difference between digital and analog information by hinting at the widespread extent to which these ideas underlie many phenomena in our world.

As is well known, individual snowflakes grow into constrained geometrical forms. These are crystals that vary in details from flake to flake but that uniformly exhibit overall hexagonal shapes and that have individual components of the crystals oriented at sixty-degree angles or multiples thereof. This is a reflection of (i.e., is determined by) the shape of the building blocks of the snowflake, water molecules. In a sense, the water molecule is exercising digital informational control over the formation of the snowflake, using the integers of 6 and 60.

When the blanket of fallen snow has formed, however, there remains none of this digital influence. The contour of the surface of the snow blanket is not manifested by a digital description. The contour of the blanket is a variably curving one with great variability from place to place. The contours are mostly smooth curves; they are analogous to analog information.

The snow blanket contour, although highly variable, is not random. It was formed, or determined, by the variations in wind speeds and directions, which also varied a bit from location to location, as the snow fell. The contour may also come to be altered by shovels and snowplows and other forces. These forces are, in a broad sense, informational inputs governing the shape of the snow blanket. The contours of the blanket comprise a recordation of this information. The information is analog. The digital information that began the snowflake has now been subsumed under the analog snow blanket.

Rather than being termed an analogy for the difference between the two information types, this snow blanket picture might better be classified as a figure of speech called a simile. In any case, it may be helpful in visualizing how DNA loses direct control over most of cellular functioning.

When we add the effects of deterministic chaos (discussed in Chapter 9) that develops when cells become cancerous, trying to control or cure the cancer by tinkering with DNA can be seen as similar to trying to control the contour of the fallen snow by altering some of the details of snowflakes.

E.   CAN YOU LIVE FOR FIVE HUNDRED YEARS?

One of the most outlandish ideas occurring in contemporaneous times is that of enabling a marked expansion of a possible lifetime for humans. This is not a widely held idea, but there are educated people who apparently actually consider it a very reasonable one. Indeed, some believe it almost surely will come true and in the not-too-distant future. This is not a feasible possibility, for reasons I mention below.

Although the basic control mechanisms of DNA are very simple and easily understood, as we have seen in this chapter (and as will become even more clear in Chapter 9), this can be very misleading. Cellular biochemical processes develop a very complex system that slips beyond direct DNA control. The complexity underlying most biologic dynamics becomes dauntingly difficult to discern completely. This is especially relevant to the very fundamental complexity underlying the development and aging of the more complex multicellular life forms.

The developmental processes for a more complex multicellular organism (e.g., an animal) are a profoundly fundamental part of the organism, and this is relatively easy to comprehend. An animal begins life as a single cell. This cell must divide and divide again and again to grow into the animal. More important, as these cells divide, they must be transformed into the numerous different types of cells that make up the various tissues, organs, and structures of the fully grown animal.

And these structures must develop in precisely the right locations as this process proceeds. The developmental process actually lasts for the lifetime of the animal. We often tend to think that development ceases when the animal reaches adult size, but this is not quite true. Some parts of developmental change (e.g., complex neural organization in the brain) continue to develop for substantial times. Such processes slow down substantially but do not sharply end. Changes in the body eventually take on the character of regression as the body ages, but the overall picture of development and aging is a seamless one of unrelenting change. This has the flavor of being such a profound part of life as to be included within the concept of life itself.

As a part of life, the aging component of development has an even more bedrock-foundational function within life. This can be appreciated from an evolutionary perspective. All life is founded upon and springs from the process of evolution. An indispensable part of the evolution of multicellular life forms is natural selection. Natural selection, operating via "survival of the fittest," *absolutely* requires a limited and relatively short life span for individual organisms. Animals must be born, develop, reproduce, and then die in order for natural selection to work. This means that aging and dying are built into the structure of life. They are built into the structure in a way that is so integral and fundamental as to be indispensable. It's more than just being "built into our genes." They are also built into our epigenetics and our biochemistry and physiology. Death is built into life.

Nevertheless, there are some molecular biologic findings that have given researchers optimism about being able to halt the aging and dying processes. For example, there is knowledge about correlates between cellular aging and chromosomal structures called telomeres. A telomere is a short segment of DNA that is found at the end of the long chromosomal DNA strands. The telomeres are repeated about fifty times at each end. As a rough analogy, the telomere groups at the ends of a chromosome can be thought of as something like bookends. They serve some type of protective function. When a chromosome is duplicated for the purpose of cell division, the process entails the sacrifice of a bit of DNA at the chromosomal end; a telomere is snipped off and lost. After about fifty cell divisions, the telomeres are almost all lost, and this seems to interfere with the ability of the cell to divide further. The cell has become old in this sense and is at the end of its reproductive life.

There is an enzyme called telomerase, however, that is capable of forming new telomeres. The optimistic hope, therefore, is that somehow telomerase can be engineered to enable all the cells of the body to have the capacity to renew their telomere ends and thereby prevent cellular aging and dying. This sounds relatively simple. In all likelihood, however, the task of actually being able to control such processes will prove to be intractable. This is because the relevant analog informational controls over cellular processes almost surely have some chaotic qualities. (Deterministic chaos and its importance will be discussed in Chapter 9.) This means that the effort to try to control or mitigate aging will have some adverse unintended and unpredictable consequences. Evidence for this claim can be found in one aspect of cancer. Cancer cells have developed the capacity to use telomerase in such a way as to prevent the shortening of their telomere strands. This is one factor that helps allow the cancer cells to continue to proliferate without limit, which is one of the fundamental qualities that makes a cancer a cancer.

Tinkering with telomeres is unlikely to bring about useful increases in life span. Trying to alter factors such as this one will likely have unintended adverse consequences that far outweigh any beneficial effect. These adverse consequences will likely occur because, again, dying is so integrated into the fabric of life as to be surely tinker-proof.

There is evidence that the human life span is limited to about 115 years. One can discern this through examining Figure 7. The average life spans for people in developed countries has increased markedly in the latter portions of the modern age, but the maximum life span has not. In ancient times, even though most people died relatively young, a few very lucky persons lived to be about as old as the oldest people living today. The main reason so many people died much sooner than their programmed life span was that they were very vulnerable to the many diseases that they had no control over, especially infectious diseases.

There are rare reports of individuals supposedly living decades longer than 115 years. These reports, however, have very poor or essentially absent documentation available to substantiate the age claims. If a few rare persons actually have lived significantly longer than 115 years, these are such extremely rare occurrences as to be anomalies. Their import for the point being made about an inherently limited life span is very questionable.

Problems with understanding information theory, as detailed in this chapter, have led to much ill-founded optimism about progress in fields of biology and medicine. This degree of optimism will likely prove to be utopian. These problems related to information theory also extend to biologic fields other than DNA and molecular biology, as we will see in the following chapters.

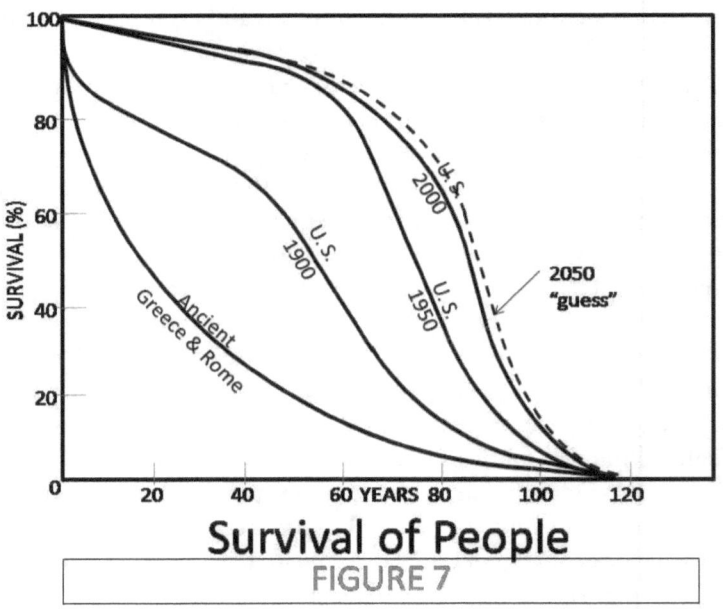

Survival of People

FIGURE 7

Chapter 7

The Digital Delusion of Neurophysiology

Over a half century ago, when I was in college, I sensed a high level of excitement among some people about devices that they called computers. The business school at the university had just acquired a huge computer that operated using vacuum tubes. There were so many of these tubes that the collective heat that they generated was truly enormous. The computer required the continuous operation of a large air-cooling system. I was told that if the cooling system should suddenly fail, the computer would melt within about a minute.

To give you another idea of how primitive this computer was, the total memory capacity was two thousand bits, or 250 bytes, although the word "byte" had not yet been contrived. Nevertheless, this early computer was very exciting for some people.

In learning about this computer, I perceived the first glimmers of the essence of digital information processing. Not long after, I also detected faint glimmers of another exciting field that seemed to have some relationship to the computer, although it was indeed a different field. This was the field of neurophysiology, a part of "brain science." The reason for telling you about these early days of long ago is to give you an appreciation of the long time period over which my ideas discussed below developed. A long time period over which to examine something can give one a valuable point of perspective not available from a shorter, more limited experience.

Subsequently, I learned more about neurophysiology in medical school. It was then that that I had the occasions to experience the striking phenomenon that led to one of the most insidious and long-lasting misconceptions to arise within a modern day scientific field. The striking phenomenon is the visual representation of the activity of nerve cells (neurons) as seen displayed on an oscilloscope screen. An oscilloscope is a cathode ray tube (CRT) device that displays the details of the shapes and timing of electrical signals of some type. It has some similarity to a television display, and indeed, televisions utilized CRTs until recently.

Neurophysiologists doing basic research used oscilloscopes to display nerve activity as they performed various experimental studies. If you have never experienced seeing such activity displayed upon an oscilloscope, I will try to describe it, although it is difficult to convey in words the exciting intensity of the experience. It is especially impressive if the oscilloscope also has an audio amplifier that can make sounds timed to the nerve activity. Neurons fire a short spurt or pulse of electrical activity called a neuronal or axonal spike. The spike represents a current traveling across the nerve membrane. It is generated at the main body of the nerve, but numerous experiments have shown that this current impulse actually travels from the main body along the main nerve fiber, called the axon, to the end of the axon. Axons can be surprisingly long. The spike is of very short duration at any one point on the axon, but it has considerable amplitude. It looks like a sword sticking straight up when displayed on the oscilloscope screen. When the oscilloscope also has an audio amplifier, the sound effect from a series of spikes is sharp, staccato popping sounds. The combined effect of both the visual and auditory display is captivating.

The nerve spike is an "all-or-none" phenomenon. That is, the nerve either fires the fully formed spike or does nothing at all. Either the input stimuli to the neuron that cause it to fire spikes reach a threshold for firing or they don't. For a given short interval, the neuron—or more formally, its axon—is either on or off.

Does this on and off quality have a familiar ring to it when you think of the discussion about digital information in the last chapter? If not, let me add something. In seeing and hearing a nerve spike train, you certainly will readily realize that the spikes can be counted. The spikes are discrete; that is, they are point-like rather than being a continuous form of activity. Surely, then, this activity must be a form of digital information representation. This was the conclusion of virtually everyone who experienced these parameters of nerve activity. Those who also knew a bit about how computers worked concluded that the nervous system, including the brain, was like a computer—that is, the brain utilized and processed digital information. Since computers were quite readily understandable, then the brain should be also.

I recall these ideas circulating in the 1960s. I also recall my having a vague feeling, however, that there might be something just slightly askew or troubling about this comparison of the brain with a computer. I wasn't sure what the basic problem might be, however, and this was not really important to me because it was not related to my professional interests and activities.

Gradually, however, over some years, the cause of the troubling feeling I had about whether the brain was really a digital information processor became clear to me. The answer is no; the brain is an analog processor. The belief on the part of others that it was digital was a delusion. What intrigued me the most for many years was that I was not aware of anyone else who realized this fundamental error. There are now professional brain scientists, however, who finally have recognized this error, and I now can take satisfaction in this evidence that I was correct.

For most readers, my explication of the reasons for why the brain is not a digital information processing system will be difficult to grasp. But the effort will be worth a try because the example is such a powerful one for our purpose. There are two main reasons that it is powerful. First, the example shows how extensively the scientific community can be off base and also that such an error can last a surprisingly long time within the community. Second, it is a demonstration of the surprising extent to which such an error can engender false optimism about the rate of progress that is expected in science. This brain science example is a good one for showing how progress can be much more limited than scientists predict.

The first hint for the answer to the cause for the digital delusion regarding the brain is found by observing the time intervals between nerve spikes or pulses. While the pulse frequency may seem almost constant for a short period, it is clearly not perfectly so. Over longer periods, depending on the details of the experiment being done, the pulse frequencies change markedly. Sometimes there are unexpected bursts of very frequent spikes. Whether these episodic changes are slight or are very pronounced, one gets the perception that the intervals between pulses can have any duration. That is, the spectrum of possible interval lengths is a continuous one. The lengths of the intervals cannot be expressed by integers. Thus, spike frequencies do not encode digital information.

But which is important for information transfer in the brain, the countable occurrences of spikes across the oscilloscope screen or the continuously variable intervals between the spikes? This question is the crucial one. The answer can be found by thinking about what happens after the nerve spike reaches the end of the nerve axon. Near its end, the axon divides into multiple branches. Each of the branches connects to another neuron. The information carried by the nerve spike is thus passed on to multiple other neurons.

I said that the axon branch *connects to* another neuron, but this is not quite true. At the end of the branch, there is a small structure called a synapse. Across the center of the synapse is a very thin space, or gap, that actually forms a disconnect between the one neuron and the next in line. There is not quite a true connection between the structures of the two neurons in the sense of a continuous, uninterrupted path. The information carried by the axonal spike must somehow jump this gap.

This happens by the electrical signal of the spike being converted into a purely chemical signal. Chemical compounds called neurotransmitters are released at the end of the axonal branch into the synaptic gap. The transmitter molecules travel across the gap and are picked up at the synaptic receiving end. This receiving end of the synapse is in a branching part, called a dendrite, of the next (receiving) neuron. It is in this process that the features of axonal spikes suggesting a possible digital nature to neural information transfer are lost. Clearly the information in the gap is analog information. It is analog because it cannot be represented by an integer count.

There are many who will argue that there are structures or entities involved in the gap-jumping process that can be counted. For example, the neurotransmitter molecules in the axonal (transmitting) portion of the synapse are stored in little sacs called vesicles, and these vesicles would be countable. There are several problems with this idea. The vesicles are ruptured and disappear in the process of releasing the transmitter molecules into the synaptic gap. It is these molecules that carry the information across the gap. Second, there is no feasible mechanism known that could count or register the process of vesicle disruption.

What about counting the transmitter molecules as a substitute for counting the vesicles the molecules were stored in? Molecules are individual particles that could be counted. There are individual transporting channels (ion channels) at the receiving end of the synapse, in the dendrite of the next neuron. These channels are where the transmitter molecules enter and affect the receiving neuron. The channels have features that cause them to function in a "gated" manner (the technical details are voltage gating and ligand gating). This gating characteristic might cause some to suggest that the channel is analogous to an on-off switch, that the channel could represent digital information. This argument goes nowhere for several reasons. The opening and closing of a channel have a stochastic (probabilistic) dynamic that would prevent the stable, latching quality required for a digital switch. The operation of these channels results in dendritic membrane voltage changes that are integrated (summed) over the involved area of the dendritic membrane. This membrane is a continuous structure, and the voltage summations represent a continuous (i.e., analog) variable. The information encoded by this voltage is therefore analog information. The opening and closing of an ion channel is not counted or recorded in any way.

The other problem with a theoretical counting of transmitter molecules as a mechanism of representing the information the molecules are carrying is the problem of signal-to-noise ratios. If one were to hypothesize that a molecule count done by the receiving dendrite could be an accurate reflection of the preceding occurrence of an axonal spike in the transmitting neuron, this argument would not hold. The vesicles that were disgorged by the occurrence of the spike contain roughly five thousand neurotransmitter molecules per vesicle. But this is an average. The vesicles vary (randomly) in volume by about 10 percent, or by about five hundred transmitter molecules. These variations represent a huge noise source with respect to a hypothesized counting of molecules. In other words, if one molecule were to represent a bit of information, then random occurrences (noise) as great as five hundred molecules would completely overwhelm any information encoded into one molecule. Noise in the synaptic gap would be increased by the fact that some transmitter molecules are lost (e.g., they diffuse away) on their way toward a postsynaptic ion channel.

There are other arguments about digital versus analog brain processing that can arise, but perhaps we have done about enough for our purpose. One last area, however, I can't resist at least mentioning because it is an example of how nonrealistic some ideas can be. A few wayward individuals have argued that the brain may be a digital computer on a quantum physical level. The size scale, however, upon which quantum theory becomes relevant is so many orders of magnitude smaller than the scale upon which rest the biologic structures we are dealing with (transmitter vesicles, ion channels, etc.) that the arguments make no sense. Rather than trying to comment further on the difficult aspects of quantum theory that speak to why the arguments make no sense, I will simply add the following two sentences. The most excellent quantum physicist, Richard Feynman, stated that "no one really understands quantum theory." Those people who think that quantum theory can be applied to the questions of brain function do not understand that they don't understand what they are talking about.

If the digital counting of neuronal spikes does not account for information processing by the brain, what mechanism does? The answer is the timing of the spikes, the interspike intervals and the changes in those intervals. When a neuron produces spikes, it is not simply "on" during a spike but is on at varying rates depending upon the spike-firing rate. And the firing rate is an analog variable. Likewise, when it is not firing a spike, it is "off" to variable degrees depending upon how far below firing threshold the axonal membrane voltage is. Most neurons have input signals from thousands of other neurons. These inputs influence the membrane voltage of the neuron being sent the signals. These individual, tiny input signals sum in an analog fashion. The total input sum could vary anywhere from zero up to the firing threshold membrane voltage. If the membrane voltage is near zero, it would take a large additional signal to cause it to fire, but if it were already near threshold, firing would require only a tiny additional input. Thus, the neuron can be "off" to variable extents and is not simply a two-state binary switch.

The faster that input signals come in, the closer the receiving neuron is to firing. And after threshold is reached, an increase in rate of input signals causes an increase in the firing rate of the receiver's axon. Thus, the rates of firing seem to be the information-encoding mechanism. Much experimental evidence of various types supports this idea that the timing of spike activity of numerous neurons acting in concert is the way the brain does what is does. These timing and synchronizing qualities of brain activity are continuously variable. And this is very unlike a digital computer.

Having argued that information processing in the brain is not based upon digital information, I now must go back and make a slight modification to this assertion in the interests of completeness and the fact that some will probably still argue with my claims. I go back to the description of oscilloscope displays of neuronal activity. Recall that the displays of spike trains, both visually and auditorally, produce an overwhelming impression of digital information processing. For those readers who might remain haunted by this strong impression, I must confess that, in a limited way, your impression probably has some validity. For signal transport down a single nerve axon, the signal transfer does seem to have a digital quality. This digital quality is important for maintenance of a reliable signal while it is transferred over a long neuron. Some axons are surprisingly long. Information that travels along a long axon would be subject to some degradation.

The signal degradation would come from two main sources. First, there could be changes in axonal membrane voltage over appreciable distances. Examples of signal transfer in other devices that would be analogous are as follows. An electric current flowing through a wire has an associated voltage drop due to resistance in the wire. A radio signal, even if it is focused into a beam at the transmitter end, loses power with distance. This is why some electrical or electromagnetic signal transfers include periodic amplifying stations along the way. A second signal degradation factor would be membrane noise. A nerve membrane maintains a voltage across it for purposes of its required function as an electrical signal producer. This voltage is produced by biochemical mechanisms that transport ions across the membrane. There are random membrane voltage fluctuations because of thermal effects, chemical influences, and other causes, including processes occurring outside the cell itself. Random membrane voltage fluctuations operating over long distances could cause a significant reduction in the reliability of spike maintenance.

Many, not all, nerve axons are insulated by myelin (fatty) sheaths. There are periodic interruptions of the sheaths called nodes of Ranvier that serve several (related) functions. They are the points that enable ion transport so that the axonal membrane can maintain its voltage. They also serve as points that are analogous to periodic amplifiers along the relatively long distance that many axons must transport the information signal encoded by the electrical spike. The neural spike is "rejuvenated" in the process of jumping across the node of Ranvier. This process is usually described as allowing for faster transport of the nerve signal. It does that, but I would point out that this also helps preserve the digital quality (i.e., the reliability) of the information being transported by the nerve pulse. It keeps the spike magnitude well above the level of noise influences.

The important point is, however, that this digital quality of the signal is entirely limited to the axonal travel. When the signal goes from the axonal ends to the dendrites of the next neuron during the process of crossing the synaptic gap, the digitality is lost. Recall that within an information processing system that has multiple steps, all of the steps must be digital or else the overall processing becomes analog.

The issues that have been discussed are difficult ones. This helps explain why the digital delusion of neurophysiology has been so widespread and ingrained. The following anecdote will emphasize this. A biological scientist won a Nobel Prize for work that was of the greatest importance and value to biology. All readers would recognize his name. During most of the rest of his career, he was involved in a biological field different from the one for which he had won the prize. This second field was brain science.

This scientist was one of the many who was captivated by the idea that the brain functioned as a digital information processor. This delusion persisted until the death of the scientist more than a third of a century later. Not surprisingly, the progress that this scientist made in the field of brain science was hardly of Nobel Prize caliber. Indeed, his accomplishments in this field, within which he spent most of his professional life, were not noteworthy. This is an example of progress being very much more limited than the prevailing optimism would predict.

The story of the digital delusion of neurophysiology is a striking example of limitations of progress in science. The limitations associated with this kind of misunderstanding can be unapparent to most. They also can be very far reaching. The far reach is indicated in the next chapter, and in a way, it is a continuation of this story about brain function.

Chapter 8
The Artificiality of Artificial Intelligence

I was a teenager at the time the field of artificial intelligence was beginning to develop. So my adult life has been concurrent with the history of this field. As I look back upon that history, I see things that are interesting and also quite relevant for our discussion in this book. Perhaps you will find them interesting also.

A reasonable definition of artificial intelligence (AI) would be "the science of making machines do things that would require intelligence if done by people" (Marvin Minsky). The beginning of AI as a modern, recognized discipline was at a two-month-long conference in 1956 at Dartmouth University involving ten people. Small groups at the Massachusetts Institute of Technology, Carnegie Institute of Technology (subsequently Carnegie-Mellon University), and Stanford University were the main centers of AI research over the following twenty-five years. Although the groups were few and were small in numbers of members, they were relatively well funded, especially through the Defense Advanced Research Projects Agency (DARPA) of the Department of Defense (DoD). The researchers were a very enthusiastic bunch with grandiose expectations and wondrous predictions of what their endeavors would accomplish. Briefly, the early predictions included automated language translation within a short period of time, a computer world chess champion within a decade, and computers and robots that essentially could do human-level thinking within a decade or two and that would surpass humans thereafter.

There were reasons for this grandiose enthusiasm. There were oversimplified ideas about how the brain worked. Partly, this was a result of the influential behaviorist school of psychology that emphasized the idea of simple reflexes as underlying all behavior. This was greatly compounded by the digital delusion of neurophysiology discussed in the last chapter. The epitome of intellectual functions was thought to be mathematics and symbolic logic as propounded by the philosophy of logical positivism. Such functions seemed eminently well suited to being enacted by computers. During World War II, computers had played an important role in breaking cryptographic codes, and automated language translation was thought to be an analogous process that computers could be programmed to do. This idea was enhanced by the ideas of Noam Chomsky, who held that the important part of language was syntax (structure) rather than semantics (meaning). To me, this seems like a peculiar point of view, but Chomsky's ideas were very influential. Finally, the public press played a part in helping to make the predictions about thinking machines even more newsworthy by embellishing the already grandiose predictions.

In the 1960s, some progress was made. Although chess programs evolved more slowly than had been predicted, they did so steadily. Some progress was made in "search tree" limitation. (Search trees occur in the solving of many problems and consist of the computer's searching for an answer by computing along a path that branches into multiple computing pathways, and those branches further branch, then those branches branch, and so on. Search trees are a problem because often the number of branches is astronomical or even infinite.) Quite a bit of effort was devoted to computerized vision, and programs were developed that could do something akin to rudimentary seeing.

Lack of progress and failures, however, were more prominent and characteristic of the 1960s than was the meager progress. Computer vision related only to a very highly constrained, rigidly defined, and limited environment. It had nothing remotely approaching the subtleties and the interpretive marvels of human vision. DARPA-funded robotics and autonomous mobile vehicle projects that might have military field applications required a lot of research work directed at computerized vision. These projects, however, fell far short of DoD expectations, and it looked like significant progress was not going to be made. The projects essentially were cancelled in the early 1970s.

Search tree limitation was still a significant problem. The brain is very good at choosing from the outset the few or single best search paths and ignoring others. Not much is known about how the brain does this, but it is a necessary feature of efficient functioning of the intelligent brain. For AI researchers, this remained a formidable obstacle.

It is interesting that mental functions that are considered among the highest of intellectual functions, such as mathematics and symbolic logic formulations, are the things that computers can do with relative ease, whereas many of the things that we do automatically and with little or no thinking, such as perception and language communication, have proven to be almost insurmountable problems for the computer modeling of intelligent behavior. The brain is mostly not logical, at least if compared to formal logic systems.

Trying to put knowledge into a computer has proven to be another formidable challenge, especially when it is common sense knowledge about the world. Consider what the computer would need to know to adequately answer the following apparently simple word problem. If a young man can go into the woods and pick eight baskets of berries in a day and a sexually attractive young woman can pick seven baskets in a day, how many baskets will they pick if they go into the deep, dark woods together as a team? A moment's reflection will indicate that there is more than one possible answer to this question, and the computer might even need a sense of humor to completely cover the answers.

Regarding automated language translation, forty-five years ago I first heard the following example of computerized language translation. If an English sentence were translated into Russian and then that translation were back-translated into English by the same computer program, one should end up with the same or nearly the same sentence as the starting one. An example of the type of result that happened with attempts at automated translation is as follows: Input sentence—"The spirit is willing, but the flesh is weak." Output (back-translation): "The vodka is good, but the meat is spoiled." Obviously, automated language translation poses daunting problems.

With the significant failures of the 1960s and the subsequent major decrease in DoD funding, the 1970s were a relatively slow period for AI research, although some progress was made. There was a trend to pay more attention to how the brain does things. Most of our behavioral decisions are quick, subconscious, automatic ones not derived from deep thinking or reasoning. Reasoning takes time, and the survival value for an animal of *not* reasoning is obvious. These automatic decisions are, however, based upon considerable *knowledge* about the world, either instinctual or learned. Accordingly, there came a period when the development of computerized algorithms known as "expert systems" were begun. Expert systems are based on "teaching" the computer a large fund of knowledge of the type that an expert in a specialized field has and would use to make decisions relevant to that field. Two examples developed in the 1970s are DENDRAL and EURISKO. DENDRAL was a ten-year effort to develop a program to help determine the structure of organic molecules. EURISKO (from the Greek for "I discover") was used to help design complicated things such as computer chips.

In the 1980s, AI entered the marketplace. High-level technology, or "high tech," related to a number of fields—for instance, biotechnology—was becoming popular in investment circles. This, together with the partial success of expert systems, stimulated investment and industrial activity in the field. The cost of developing expert systems decreased due to the production of systems with operating "shells" that could be filled in with customized knowledge bases and that could be tailored to specific industrial needs. By 1985, 150 companies had spent a billion dollars on in-house development of expert systems. Another example of increased activity was the fact that 100 companies offered for sale in 1985 computerized vision systems for industrial use. In the middle of the decade, there was approximately a sixteen-fold increase in the number of researchers in the field of AI. Digital Equipment Corporation (DEC) had seventy-seven AI researchers in 1986; in 1988, the corporation had seven hundred such people.

Fundamental problems loomed again, however. A quotation from early twentieth century physiologist Claude Bernard is apropos: "We achieve more than we know; we know more than we understand; we understand more than we can explain." Indeed, we know more than we can explain. Some of a human expert's knowledge is extraordinarily difficult to try to represent in a computer. Also, although computers at this time were faster and had much greater memories than those of the 1960s, the expert systems were mostly based upon twenty-year-old programming techniques, and some people came to believe that the systems "just made stupid decisions faster." The structure of the programming language (LISP, for LISt Processor) used for the systems became "hard" or rigid when the knowledge base was significantly expanded or updated. DEC was using an expert system called XCON (for eXpert CONfigurer) to configure advanced and very complicated computer systems. XCON originally was estimated to have replaced about 75 people, but eventually it required 150 people to keep it up and running. Although expert systems were of some value to a nonexpert, to a true expert they provided little more than reminder lists.

These problems produced a bust phase to the boom of the 1980s. Many companies foundered and went out of business. Machine Vision International crashed in 1988. General Electric, 3M Company, and others withdrew from the computer vision market. A DARPA robotics project, reinitiated earlier in the decade and termed the Automated Land Vehicle, befell the funding axe in 1989. Japan had launched its ambitious Fifth Generation Computer Project around the beginning of the decade. This was an effort based mostly on logic rather than on how the brain really works, and it fell far short of expectations.

To make the history of AI more complete, we should examine a part of that history that focused on what are called neural nets, or neural networks. This was an attempt to emulate, albeit in a limited and simplistic way, how brain neurons might process information, rather than relying solely on classical computer programming methods of step-by-step, series computations. One reason neural nets seemed to have potential is that they exhibit something that can be considered a form of learning, although so far mostly only of a rudimentary quality.

Neural nets consist of interconnected devices called units that receive input signals either from the environment or from other units. The units are arranged in groups called layers. If units receive the signals from the environment, they are in the input layer. When processing is done, the signals have reached the output layer, and this is the final result of the processing. In between the input and output layers, the processing can be made more complex with "hidden" layers. The network is very highly interconnected; that is, each unit can receive signals from many other units, and each unit can send signals to many other units.

It is the job of each unit to sum the many signals that it receives.

Then it takes the sum and performs some type of alteration of it, called an operation. Different types of operations can be performed depending on how the network is constructed. A simple operation can be thought of as just multiplying the sum by a given factor, for example, a fraction. This altering operation is usually referred to as giving "weights" to the input signals. After the weighting operation is performed, the unit then transmits the result to the units to which its output pathways are connected.

After one complete processing pass through the net is done, the weighting values can be changed for another processing pass. If the weighting changes are influenced by the output result from the previous processing pass, then this is analogous to a type of learning. The interconnection weight changes are analogous to synaptic strength changes that occur in real neurons, which are the basis for learning accomplished by real brains.

Some type of supervisory method, a training method, that examines how closely the output of the net approaches some goal, calculation, or other conclusion influences the learning process. The supervisory method then makes some changes in the weights and does the processing pass again, monitoring the result to check whether it is closer to or farther from the desired goal. Then the weights are changed again, and the process is repeated over and over. This has some similarity to negative feedback control, which is discussed in Chapter 12.

Some networks don't have supervisory feedback control for training but rather are "self-organizing" nets. The exact understanding of the details of how many nets work can become very challenging and indeed can surpass understanding. Networks may or may not "converge" to a desired learning goal. A lot of the research involves much trial-and-error testing.

Although neural nets are not a new idea, this research was earlier considered by many as only on the fringes of mainstream AI efforts. Early nets, many of which were called "perceptrons," had binary (on-off) units and, more important, were limited to two layers of units, an input and an output layer. The "in-between" layers, the hidden ones, complicated the net such that no one knew how to algorithmically (i.e., logically stepwise) change the connection weights during training so that the net would reliably converge toward, or learn, a solution to an input problem. In 1968, Marvin Minsky and Seymour Papert, two important

AI researchers at MIT, published a book that thoroughly examined the qualities of binary two-layered nets (*Perceptrons*). Among other things, they demonstrated that it was impossible for these nets to perform one of the basic logical analytic functions, the fundamental "exclusive-or" logical operation. This was an extreme limitation. Although it was perhaps not the authors' intention, the book was partly responsible for virtually halting neural net research for fifteen years.

In 1974, a Harvard graduate student (Paul J. Werbos) devised a method called the "back propagation algorithm" that was capable of systematically changing connection weights by increments in multilayered networks. His discovery, however, virtually went unnoticed, perhaps because its value was not realized and perhaps because only a little work was being done in the field at that time. Rumelhart and Parker rediscovered the algorithm in 1984, and it was made widely known in the field by 1986. Also, in 1982, the physicist Hopfield demonstrated that such nets were guaranteed to converge toward or learn a good solution because of a theory analogous to thermodynamic theory. These developments greatly enhanced neural net research. In 1989, three hundred companies were working in the field, with projected sales of one billion dollars by the year 2000. In 1991, there were ten thousand workers researching neural networks.

Most research on neural nets has involved simulating the nets on digital computers with the classic (von Neumann) serial processing of information through one central processing unit. When implemented as real hardware devices, however, neural nets are parallel processors, like the brain. Of course, it is well known that the brain performs many of its computations very fast even though individual neurons are very slow, compared to an electronic signal, because of the massively parallel architecture of the brain. Although digital computers with significant parallel processing capacity have been built, neural nets are more "naturally" or basically parallel. Also, like the brain, they are analog information processors, with a few exceptions. Although VLSI (very large scale integration) neural net hardware devices analogous to VLSI digital chips present design and manufacturing challenges, some progress has been made.

The exact architecture of neural nets has a great many variations, and trying to fully understand them is challenging. In fact, the processing behavior rapidly becomes highly complex as the number of interconnected units increases beyond just a few. The behavior, thus, is not fully understandable nor is it fully predictable or reliable. Networks have been developed that are useful for some practical purposes, but significant progress will probably remain challenging.

During the last two decades, enthusiasm about AI has been greatly tempered compared to what it was earlier. But this fact can't be transferred directly into a certainty that the progress curve is slowing toward a halt. Although progress in AI has been very much slower than initially expected, there has been some progress and there continues to be. Thus, progress may continue without much more slowing well into the future. This is a quite different progress curve than the rapidly reverse-bending one for the transportation revolution. How far the progress in AI may eventually go and when that progress may tend toward an ending cannot be predicted with any reliability. There are several things that can be said, however, that relate to limits for AI.

First, as we have shown, AI progress since its beginning has been quite slow, with no evidence apparent for an increasing pace of progress. For a number of reasons, it seems extremely unlikely that there will be some major breakthrough or epiphany that would enable rapid progress. The basic aims of the field are just too challenging for that to occur. We have evidence that this kind of rapid progress is unlikely to happen in any current scientific endeavor. Theoretical developments that could render revolutionary progress easy were developed long ago. Regarding AI, science has studied the brain for centuries, and progress has never been revolutionary. Therefore, even if progress in AI should continue for a long time, the very slow rate of that progress forms a type of limitation.

A second form of limitation stems from the fact that AI will forever remain a nonhuman form of intelligence. This may not be completely obvious, but it is true in an almost axiomatic way—true by definition. Human intelligence is greatly and fundamentally informed by the experiences of an individual. These experiences range in multiple ways across the spectra of personal social interactions and broad, complex, rich cultural influences. These experiences cannot be passed from one human to another, let alone from a human to a computer—and neural nets are a type of computer. Even a very sophisticated and intelligent robot will have been made in a laboratory or a manufacturing company plant, and it will be impossible for the robot to have social and cultural experiences comparable to those of a human. It cannot, therefore, have a human intelligence (QED). Whatever intelligence it may have will forever remain artificial in that it will not be human. This is a form of limitation for AI, and it is insurmountable.

There are naïve optimists who will argue that AI devices can probably be connected to a human brain in some way that will enable the devices to become fully integrated with the brain. In this way, they could make the human more intelligent. This unrealistic idea has been partly fostered by the implantable technological devices that already have been developed and used to supply sensory inputs to a person who is deaf or blind. Also, devices have been developed that enable a person to have some brain-induced control over a paralyzed limb. These devices, however, perform functions that are vastly different from the challenges involved in trying to integrate a device into the actual cognitive functions of intelligent brain activity. Such an attempt would have to be limited in the same way that the overall strength of a chain is determined by its weakest link. If one's aim is to make a brain smarter with an AI device, then the entire brain will have to be replaced. Then, by definition, the brain is no longer human. AI will never make humans smarter than they are. This is a fundamental limit to the field.

Chapter 9
Chaotic Dynamics and Society

One of the biggest scientific-mathematical-conceptual advances in the second half of the twentieth century was the development of an understanding of deterministic chaos (chaos theory). This advance, however, has not quite received the degree of recognition it probably merits. There are some reasons for this, which will be noted later.

In the prior chapter on the limits of DNA, the argument for limits was based on information theory. Chaos also influences the limits of DNA as the digital determinism of DNA gives way to the analog processes comprising most of cellular biochemistry and the physiology of animals. The limiting effects of these two factors, chaos and information theory, differ in the following respect. It is puzzling that most scientists do not understand the fact that the digital controlling aspects of DNA fade away for most cellular dynamics. The arguments for this are not highly abstruse or dauntingly difficult. It is easy, however, to understand why most people do not appreciate deterministic chaos. Chaos is difficult to understand, and this short chapter is not sufficient to completely explain it. It is counterintuitive. It is difficult to know if it might be present in a given dynamic system. If it is present, it can be subtle and can remain "hidden." If it is perceived, it is difficult to know how to deal with it. Most of all, it flies in the face of our deeply ingrained sense of the ability of mathematics to calculate most things exactly and the ability of engineers and scientists to calculate almost everything else with only minute errors at the most.

A. The Horror of the Butterfly

Although deterministic chaos cannot be thoroughly addressed in the format of this book, a few chosen comments can serve our purpose. The "butterfly effect" is a widely known metaphor that illustrates one of the most important aspects of chaos, the extreme sensitivity to initial conditions. This means that extremely minute errors or uncertainties, or the overlooking of very tiny effects, in the input parameters or "starting points" of the dynamic system being examined can make surprisingly huge and unpredictable changes in what the system does down the line a bit. The metaphor of the butterfly conveys this idea. The metaphor is that the flapping of a single butterfly's wings somewhere in the world could end up causing a tornado on a different continent or a hurricane at sea. In a way, the metaphor is a good one for illustrating the point. It may, however, be a bit overdone. Perhaps a better one would be that a butterfly could end up affecting the timing of a storm elsewhere, with the storm having gathered mainly from causes other than those related to the butterfly's wings flapping. But even this latter statement seems fantastic and counterintuitive.

In the late nineteenth century, the excellent mathematician Henri Poincaré caught a glimpse of the essence of the butterfly effect. Although the metaphor had not been conjured at that time, Poincaré's mathematical deliberations produced some results and insights that were very much a forerunner of deterministic chaos. These perceptions were seemingly so antithetical to the "normal" mathematical concepts of the time, which entailed a beautiful mathematical precision and an elegant perfection, that Poincaré is said to have reacted in horror at the implications. The further pursuit of these concepts was abandoned, and the concepts mostly remained dormant and unapparent for another three quarters of a century.

For our purposes, the butterfly metaphor, although essentially valid, has the potential disadvantage of seeming too fantastic. Most people would feel that it is so removed from common experience that, although it might theoretically be valid, it can essentially safely be ignored for all practical purposes. In this way, it would resemble quantum mechanics.

Quantum mechanics, however, is so far apart from the larger world in which we live that it indeed can be ignored for most purposes. Chaos, on the other hand, very much exists in our everyday world, although it is not obvious. The extent of its importance somewhat remains to be determined, but it is probably very common. It shows up in unexpected places, and sometimes it is important. For example, the basic equations of ecology that describe animal population dynamics are simple. Yet, chaotic effects can greatly alter populations from the numbers expected from using these equations. This has profoundly affected some aspects of ecology. We cannot afford to ignore chaos; the wings of the horrible butterfly are present in our world. Perhaps chaos could be viewed as the Heisenberg uncertainty principle of quantum theory for our everyday (macroscopic) world as opposed to the subatomic world.

B. *Chaos Is Insidious*

In addition to extreme sensitivity to initial conditions, chaotic systems have three other characteristics: (1) they are deterministic, (2) they are aperiodic, and (3) they are bounded. These characteristics are important to give an understanding to the quality or "flavor" of chaos. I will briefly describe some aspects of these characteristics.

The behaviors of chaotic systems are "determined" by their descriptive mathematical equations. These equations usually are in the class called nonlinear differential equations. For our purposes, the importance of this type of equation is two-fold. First, nonlinear equations usually cannot be explicitly—that is, mathematically perfectly—solved. Answers can be approximated by using an iterative process (repeated calculations) that takes an approximate solution to readjust some numbers in the equation. The equation is then solved again and this answer will be better, although still not perfect. The process is repeated over and over using computers to get better and better approximations. But the answer will never be perfect. The second problem with attempting a solution for a nonlinear equation describing a dynamic system is the fact that the starting points of the system, which are the input values used to calculate the approximate answer to the equation, require physical measurements. Even though measurements can usually be made highly precise, they are never perfect. For most purposes, measurements are "good enough." But for systems that prove to be chaotic, even a miniscule error in the measurement of a starting value can result, after some time, in a huge error in the predicted behavior of the system. These solutions become highly inaccurate in the longer term, and as a consequence the system becomes highly unpredictable in the longer term. This has been a very surprising, and very important, characteristic of chaos.

A characteristic of chaos that adds to the sense of unpredictability is its aperiodicity. In general, predictable, orderly dynamic systems occur in only a surprisingly few types. Aside from episodic transient behaviors, there are only two categories of such orderly system behaviors: steady-state behavior and periodic behaviors. Periodic behaviors are oscillatory; they are perfectly repeated at regular intervals. A majority of behaviors examined by classical physics and much of practical technical-engineering applications are of this type. Chaos is not steady state, but any repetitions are not at regular intervals, nor are they perfect repetitions. Thus, aperiodicity adds to the unpredictable quality of chaotic dynamics.

Therefore, because of the unpredictability and the aperiodicity of chaotic systems, they manifest a type of disorder. Chaotic systems seem "wild." For this reason, many people equate chaos with being random. This is a mistake, however. In this respect, "chaos" is a misleading term for the behaviors we are addressing. This is the reason that chaos is sometimes labeled "deterministic chaos" to emphasize that it is neither random nor completely wild. The characteristic of being bounded emphasizes this. The behavior of the system is such that it tends to be drawn toward an area of behavior, what is called the "strange attractor." The strange attractor keeps the behavior in bounds; it prevents complete wildness or randomness. Chaos is deterministic and bounded, but it is difficult—actually, impossible—to determine the behavior perfectly in the longer run.

The determinism means that the behavior is relatively predictable in the shorter term. The boundedness indicated by the strange attractor means that it is not completely wild. Also, although it is aperiodic, it can exhibit a quasiperiodicity. Thus, chaos can be and indeed usually is unapparent. Its presence can be very hidden. Chaos has been described as "a form of order disguised as disorder." This is fair, but I would also note the opposite, which may be more revealing of the insidious character of chaos: it is a form of disorder disguised as order. That is why it can be so hidden or unapparent. This aspect, together with our common reluctance to recognize an important disorder in our ordinary Newtonian world, allows chaos to go unappreciated by most. We don't want our world to be disorderly.

In oversimplified descriptions of chaos, it is often said to be "between order and disorder." This is a bit misleading in that it suggests that chaos has ordinary characteristics midway on a linear scale. Chaos is a different animal and, just as the Cheshire cat, is elusive, and it mistakenly may be assumed to be a mirage.

C. THE LIMITING EFFECTS OF CHAOS

Chaos theory was essentially rediscovered (remember the initial glimpses by Poincaré) by meteorologist-mathematician Edward Lorenz in the 1960s. Chaotic dynamics are important in weather behavior. It may be useful to comment how weather prediction has progressed during the last half century. For older readers, it may be helpful to try to recall weather forecasting from several decades ago. In doing so, it might seem that weather forecasting has made a lot of progress. I think, however, that a large part of this perception may be due to the fact that data from widely scattered regions is gathered more easily and the presentations by forecasters on TV have become more visually appealing. But there are some fundamental limits to forecasting that have not progressed much. It should be noted that we are talking about forecasting of daily details of weather. This is different from trying to say something about seasonal changes or longer-term changes, such as climate changes.

The technical improvements for visual presentation on TV are an advance, and I don't mean to belittle them. The details of these presentations in a given region can be quite useful. When a storm is affecting a small region, the forecasters can present current pictures of details that vary over short distances. Also, the forecasting of these details over ten minutes or an hour or two and the moving visual simulations of such can be helpful to local residents.

The forecasting of local weather, however, has some limitations. For example, forecasting for any highly specific location—your home, for example—becomes more and more uncertain as the area of the location becomes smaller. Forecasting for more than a week or ten days in advance becomes so uncertain as to be almost useless. Improvement in this time frame has not advanced much over the recent decades. Although more data is available faster, this increasingly manifests a highly diminishing return rate. The reason for this is chaos. And this limit upon forecasting will not improve significantly in the future. These limits are not terribly important in a practical way, but they are a good illustration of chaos. Chaos clearly is limiting, and it is a feature of our world.

D.   THE DISADVANTAGES OF IGNORING CHAOS

As an example of the potential problems that can occur when chaos goes unrecognized, I refer back to the chapter on the discussion of the looming problems for progress in cancer therapy presented by the nature of DNA in the context of cell biochemistry. Chaos further compounds the problem. Chaos is probably present to some degree in normal cell dynamics. Normal cell internal mechanisms seem to exist on the edge of chaos, likely for important biological reasons. One reason is the need for the changes that occur as cells differentiate into (i.e., change into) different cell types as development proceeds. It is well known that humans and all other animals begin as a single cell, the fertilized egg or zygote. But as the embryo and later fetus continue to grow, this original cell needs to change into a multitude of different types of cells in order to make up the different tissues and organs of the body. This ability for cells to change probably requires that an incipient instability be a basic part of the nature of the cells. This near-instability is likely related to the control systems in cells that are termed epigenetic. These are mechanisms that are not controlled by the digital determinism of DNA (i.e., they are not genetic), but the control settings nevertheless are passed on to daughter cells, analogous to DNA being passed to daughter cells. Epigenetic mechanisms are not highly stable, so they don't have digital stability. The plasticity in these control systems is required for the cells to be malleable for purposes of cell adaptability and tissue differentiation.

Chaos is almost surely present in, and an important feature of, cancer cells. This is because genetic instability seems to underlie all cancer. Instability is not synonymous with chaos, but it probably makes chaos more likely. The instability associated with cancer probably easily pushes the cell dynamics into the chaotic realm. Chaos likely increases the adaptability of cancer cells, and they can adapt to different surrounding environments (i.e., they can grow fast, spread, and metastasize). They can adapt to and become resistant to some types of treatment. Chaos likely contributes to the tissue and cell variations (heterogeneity) seen in different cancers of the same basic type and even within a given single tumor.

Most people, including even many doctors, tend to think of a given tumor diagnosis—for example, moderately differentiated adenocarcinoma of the colon—found in one person as being essentially the same as the identical diagnosis given when a tumor is found in another person. But this is a bit misleading. A surgical pathologist who spends his time looking at the cellular and organizational features of such tumors under a microscope develops a different perspective. The cells vary in multiple features from tumor to tumor and even within the same tumor from location to location. Some of the cells are very strange and ugly looking. Some are so abnormal as to appear unique in their details. A surgical pathologist develops a perspective that surely entails something like chaos occurring in cancers.

Physicians who specialize in tumor treatments, oncologists, are aware to some degree of this heterogeneity of tumors, and they recognize a need to characterize a given tumor in more detail. For this purpose, they are attempting to utilize DNA. The wonders of the sequenced human genome will, in their optimistic hopes, solve the problems of tumor heterogeneity. Thus, tumors are becoming increasingly analyzed for their genetic makeup. Mostly, a few genetic markers are used. But this surely has significant limits because of the degree of tumor heterogeneity. The number of genes analyzed can be extended to great numbers by analyzing tissue microarrays for thousands of genes. But as the numbers of genes analyzed increases, the magnitude of variations from site to site increases. Also, variations occurring over time as the tumor grows increase. An element of less-than-perfect predictability— that is, something probably related to chaos—becomes apparent. The individuation of a tumor thus becomes unstable. For therapy targeted to the exact details of an individual tumor, this may prove to be a very annoying instability.

The gene analysis of tumors will probably be hindered by another factor that is not much appreciated. As mentioned, there is a tendency to think of cancers as being engendered by a relatively few altered genes. But from the perspective of someone actually looking at tumors under the microscope, this may be misleading. Many times, the nuclei of the cells, which carry the chromosomes that carry DNA, are so horribly abnormal and deformed that one knows that the chromosomes must be significantly altered and altered in different ways among different tumor nuclei. Direct analysis of tumor chromosomes confirms this impression. This huge alteration of chromosomes means that many thousands of genes are so greatly disturbed from the normal, and disturbed differently in different cells within the tumor, that there must be a chaotic dynamic occurring. And since this dynamic will change over time as the tumor grows and is treated, the unpredictability of this process makes improvements in therapy an even greater challenge. This degree of heterogeneity means that the cancer is actually composed of a huge number of slightly differing cancers. This is probably an intractable problem for targeted or tailor-made therapies. It is impossible to fully characterize the details of a cancer. The tumor cells are too variegated and too changeable. This means that therapy can never be improved to the point of being perfect. In other words, there are limits.

E. *Why Aren't You Hearing About Chaos?*

Some readers may recall at least hearing about chaos theory a decade or two ago, even if they did not learn about it in detail. But I suspect almost all readers will not have heard much if anything about it in the last decade or so. Why would that be if chaos is an important factor in the world? My guess is that it has something to do with the pessimistic quality inherent in chaos theory. Chaotic behavior is not only difficult to perceive, but when perceived it is also usually difficult or impossible to know what to do about it or how to deal with it. In other words, it is limiting. The unpredictability that becomes clear is daunting and cannot be mitigated. This is unsettling for minds that have become hooked on the notion of unstoppable progress. This is probably why chaos seems to be evolving into a dirty little secret.

F.   WHAT DOES CHAOS HAVE TO DO WITH SOCIETY OR POLITICS?

I don't know whether chaotic dynamics, which has been developed in respect to systems that can be described in a straightforward mathematical manner, can be applied in any direct way to societal dynamics. But I suspect that most probably there are implications. If a physical system that is simple, apparently constrained, and easily understood can manifest chaotic behavior, it is highly likely that systems as complex as societal ones also have some unpredictable chaotic qualities. It is already known that societal behavior is unpredictable in many respects. Some chaotic qualities likely mean that unpredictability is intractable for society and its underlying political dynamics.

Regardless of the answer to the question of how chaos may apply directly to socio-politics, there is a clear indirect effect. Chaos certainly undermines an unlimited optimism in the arena of scientific-technical progress. Since this progress has been so important in magnifying the faith in unlimited optimism throughout society, evidence of limitations for scientific-technical progress should serve to mitigate more general societal expectations for unlimited progress. Chaos is with us. Since we comprise society, chaos surely is hiding somewhere in society and within politics.

Chapter 10

The End of Physics

Some people have referred to physics as the Queen of the Sciences. There is justification for this. In the first half of the modern era, during the seventeenth and eighteenth centuries, physics clearly stands out as the primary area of progress in science, leading the revolutionary progress of the modern world. The influence of physics was prominent in both the philosophical-theoretical realm and in the more practical-technological realm. The ideas embodied in the Copernican Revolution are an example of the first realm, and the importance of Newtonian physics in supporting this revolution is obvious. The Copernican Revolution and the resulting picture of the universe, or the cosmos, was a change in worldview that was truly an enormously profound revolution. The Industrial Revolution was an outgrowth of physics, and this is an example of its huge effect in the practical-technological realm.

The field of chemistry has been of great importance in the nineteenth and twentieth centuries. But even this field has underpinnings based in physics. There is even a defined professional field called physical chemistry. Developments in biology and related medicine have been very prominent in the twentieth century, but again many of these developments can trace some roots to physics. Thus, when I present evidence that the Queen of the Sciences has entered well into the slowing phase of the progress curve, this has great impact for the thesis of this book. If the queen is limited, her entire realm is likely limited. Limited humans will never see the colors of their quarks, nor whether their quarks are undoubtedly up or definitely down. The limits of physics will be looked at from two perspectives. One is the rate of progress in theoretical physics, and the other is progress in the fruits of physics, the technological advances related to the field. We will start with the latter.

A.   FUSION OR CONFUSION?

One of the most fantastic technological advances growing out of the progress in theoretical physics during the first half of the twentieth century was the splitting of the atom. Of course, since this led not only to the development of nuclear power but also to nuclear weapons, many will say this was not a welcome advance. Nevertheless, the field is one of huge technological advance even if there have been adverse social consequences.

The splitting of the atom, or nuclear fission, led to the development of fission weapons, which was the class of the first nuclear bombs. At the same time that fission was being developed, physicists also well understood the theoretical aspects of fusion. They knew that fusion was an extremely important process, and in a very short time the fusion weapon, the hydrogen bomb, was developed.

While the technology for weapons was given priority because of the exigencies of World War II and then the beginning of the Cold War, simultaneously physicists knew that fusion had the extremely exciting potential to give mankind an unlimited source of energy. Fusion is the source of energy produced by the sun, and there seemed to be no fundamental reason why we couldn't construct miniature suns for use on Earth.

There were predictions in the late 1940s that it might be only a decade or two until we had such energy sources. The enthusiasm on the part of some very well-known scientists was extremely high, and significant governmental funding support for the projected development of fusion power became available.

It was only a short while before an announcement to the world came from the government of Argentina that the goal had been reached. Supposedly, a scientist in that country had effectively produced a net positive production of energy by a controlled fusion process. The scientist turned out to be highly misleading to the point of fraud, and this advertisement of a major technical advance was entirely false. This was a significant embarrassment for the Argentinean government.

Over the ensuing decades, applied research efforts to get the job done were strongly supported in multiple countries with the expectation that success was just around the corner. After all, the hydrogen bomb had already demonstrated how readily we could produce a large amount of energy from fusion. All we had to do then was to control the production in a manner that did not produce an explosion. We had already done that for fission reactions. The next step for fusion should be a relatively simple one.

In order to cause hydrogen nuclei to fuse (i.e., to undergo fusion), the hydrogen must be heated to extremely high temperatures of tens to hundreds of millions of degrees. Since substances (e.g., gases) expand when heated, this means that containment requires methods of generating extremely high pressures upon the material to be fused. This turned out to be an unexpectedly formidable technical challenge.

The solution appeared to be as follows. When a gas is heated to a high enough temperature and becomes sufficiently ionized, it enters a state of matter that is beyond the three familiar forms of solid, liquid, or gas. It becomes what is called a plasma, often referred to as a fourth state of matter. In this "electrified" state and when it is carrying an electrical current, it can be influenced by magnetic fields. Theoretically, the volume of the plasma can be contained by being "pressurized" by appropriate magnetic fields surrounding the plasma. This was the technical method researched, and the expectations were high that this would succeed.

After considerable effort, however, success remained frustratingly elusive. The main problem was that the plasma became "squirmy." That is, it developed increasingly variable irregularities and slipped out of the homogenous and controlled state being sought with the surrounding confining magnetic fields.

Another method of containment was tried. The extremely high intensities of light from lasers could theoretically produce the pressures required for containment of plasmas. It soon became apparent, however, that it was difficult to produce a uniformity of pressure from individual lasers being aimed at the plasma. This difficulty persisted even when the number of lasers was greatly increased and they were pointed from multiple surrounding directions. Ingenious methods were used to try to increase the uniformity of the laser energy impingement upon the plasma. But plasma squirminess persisted.

Progress refused to appear. The stubbornly uncooperative behavior of the plasma can now be seen as surely a manifestation of the consequences of chaotic dynamics, as described in the last chapter. The earlier high hopes for progress were frustrated by the chaos hidden in nature. Not only was progress much slower than had been anticipated, it seemed to be grinding to a halt.

Then in the 1980s, a new hope appeared in the form of "cold fusion." This was a hypothesis that hydrogen nuclei could be fused without having to heat them to very high temperatures. They might be fused under special conditions that have some resemblance to those within a battery. The hydrogen atoms would be present within special metals that seemed possibly to have, under the influence of electric current, the capacity to engender fusion of the hydrogen nuclei. In the process, the fusion might release abundant energy. From the outset, many scientists were skeptical. But the people proposing the ideas were indeed scientists, essentially physical chemists, who had associations with respected universities.

There were several attempts to produce cold fusion over following years, lasting over a decade, by several different people or groups. The attempts received appreciable publicity in the lay media. Needless to say, the efforts came to naught. The experiments that were done were apparently of low caliber and often were very faulty. The efforts seem to have been heavily contaminated by overly wishful thinking and resulting biases on the part of the experimenters. Some things occurred that might be considered as bordering on the unethical covering up of experimental problems.

One cannot predict the longer-term future, so perhaps controlled fusion will be obtained one day. But at the present time, efforts are essentially dead in the water. Prospects for progress are not good. This is clearly an example of anticipated progress falling way short of expectations. Within the prevailing general optimism of our time that has grown out of the anticipation of unlimited progress in both the sciences and humanities, the fusion fiasco is a stark refutation of the reality of this degree of optimism.

B. THE INFORMATION REVOLUTION

One area that optimists will point to as an example of recent marked progress is the computer revolution and the formation of the Internet. This certainly has been an area of impressive progress. During this time, computer information capacity and processing speeds have increased at exponential rates. This has contributed to our contemporary impression of the virtual absence of limits on progress. I point out, however, a number of areas of diminishing returns on this progress.

For some purposes, processing speeds and information capacities have progressed enough that further advances would not be very meaningful. If a Google search pulls up the answers to your inquiry in a tenth of a second, of what use to you would it be if the search could be done in a hundredth of a second? If you get five hundred thousand hits on your search and you only look at the first ten or twenty, of what use would it be if the search found five million hits rather than only five hundred thousand?

The easy access to a large amount of information in a short period of time has been very helpful. But increasing the amount of information further has two big limitations. First, the further increases will likely have information of increasingly dubious or even misleading value. The best information is probably already available. Second, the information usually has to enter a human brain at some point to be useful. The brain certainly has its limits. Is your reading speed going to increase markedly?

There are a large number of technological aspects of the information revolution that would tend to be looked upon as advances but that actually are of only meager import. Is tweeting really an advance? Should texting, which most people can't resist doing while driving, be considered progress? In health care, improved management of information is supposed to make the system much more efficient. However, my daughter, who is a nurse and who is adept with computer usage, tells me that the systems that are being developed more often seem to have negative effects on her ability to do her job efficiently. This is an example of how it is becoming more difficult to make significant progress in software developments. How often have you experienced the latest operating system or application program as being less than a great improvement?

An important aspect of computer progress is that it has occurred upon theoretical advances that were accomplished about a half century ago. The technology has improved in details, but there is not much in the way of new technology based upon theoretical advances. This is important because the improvements based on making transistor switches smaller and faster certainly are approaching some physical limits. Some people have theoretical ideas about revolutionary new foundations for computing, but it is questionable how realistic these ideas are.

C. THEORETICAL-TECHNOLOGICAL DIVORCE

The fact that computer technology is based upon theory that is relatively old is an example of a very important phenomenon that I perceive to have manifested in the second half of the twentieth century. This is the tendency for theoretical progress to become increasingly separated from having relevance to practical-technological progress.

Theoretical physicists have increasingly probed farther into two realms, the realms of the unimaginably large and the unfathomably small. The questions examined are either cosmological ones or in the field of particle physics. These are exciting realms to explore, and they directly relate to the two most major advances in physics in the earlier part of the century—general relativity and quantum physics.

General relativity mostly deals with physical questions on an astronomically large scale, and quantum physics relates to those in an almost unreachably miniscule one. Since they both presumably describe the real world in some way, they should be in some manner compatible. But when attempts to combine them are made, it doesn't work. They need to be combined for some purposes. For example, to try to explain the miniscule—actually, vanishing—size of a black hole with its enormous gravity, the two theories of the small and the large both come into play. At the beginning of the cosmos or universe, the two theories likewise are needed. But they don't work together. Calculations using both theories together result in infinities and "singularities" that are not acceptable as explanations for the real world.

There has been a long attempt by twentieth-century physicists to solve this problem, that is, to formulate a theory that is capable of uniting relativity and quantum theory. This ideal theory is often referred to as the theory of everything (TOE). In the 1970s, but even more so in the 1980s, a basic theory about the nature of matter, as well as forces and spatial dimensions, began to be developed that was called string theory, and later more formally called superstring theory. These ideas are very exciting because they may have the potential to result in the TOE. There has been an embellishment called M-theory. The M stands for, among other possible things, "membrane," and sometimes the resulting concepts are referred to with the abbreviation "branes."

These theories do seem exciting, even to a novice outsider like myself. The reason they can appeal even to me is that I can begin to sense, even if I don't fully understand, that they have the potential for removing the insanity of quantum theory. I say "insanity" because quantum theory is indeed very illogical and nonsensical in a number of ways. For example, quantum theory indicates that a single particle can be in two different locations simultaneously and that a particle can arrive at a destination before it leaves its starting point. There are numerous other unfathomable contradictions. You will naturally say that this simply means that the theory must be wrong. But the theory has received very extensive experimental verification.

String theory has the potential for resolving these insane contradictions. This would be a very great theoretical advance. There are, however, several reasons to temper enthusiasm. Technological limits, at least at the present time, make experimental testing of the theory dauntingly difficult. There is hope among physicists that such limits may be partly breached. One hope is connected with the Large Hadron Collider in Geneva. The building of this facility was completed in the fall of 2008, but shortly afterward an electrical failure caused major damage. The facility was off line for more than a year, but physicists have begun exciting experiments in 2010. Among the experiments are ones that may give some support to string theory ideas. But progress will likely fall short of most hopes. We'll see. If significant experimental support and/or observational evidence for string theory cannot be obtained because of technical limitations, theoreticians will have come full circle to a very old philosophical problem, the problem of epistemology. Epistemology asks questions about what we can know and how it is that we know it. If physicists cannot adequately support string theory, how will they know that it has validity? How will they know that they know? Moreover, how will they know that they know that they know? Et cetera, *ad infinitum.*

More relevant to our discussion is the point that string theory is very unlikely to result in practical relevance or any technological progress. This is a prime example of theory having gone beyond anything of relevance to your life, now or even in the future.

A final comment on string theory will give a viewpoint that shows how, in a very fundamental and perhaps philosophical way, theoretical physics must be heading toward an ending. String theory, and its brane theory cousin, is the only thing being worked on that has any potential for significant theoretical progress. The exciting possibility that it proffers is the TOE. Either theoreticians will succeed or they won't. If they don't, this will be limiting for the field. But if they do succeed, this also will bring progress to a halt. Once you have a theory of everything, there is no challenge left to surmount.

If the Queen of the Sciences is coming to an end, what does this portend for other aspects of science? If wonderful physics is facing an inevitable limit, what does this imply for frail, biologically vulnerable man and his related humanistic endeavors? As part of the humanistic endeavors, politics and political progress likely have some limitations. The next chapter will expand upon this.

Chapter 11
The Best Political Attitude

Having given evidence that scientific progress is limited more so than most people think, we now turn to examining the meaning this may have for political attitudes. Our focus will be on the Western world, and mostly on political implications for the United States.

Although the two cultures of science and humanities exist and there are separations between them, surely there are some linkages and influences between and among disciplines. Therefore, evidence that scientific progress is fundamentally limited suggests that there may be similar fundamental limits in the socio-politico-economic realms. If political philosophies and ideas about best social conduct and societal governance have been debated and have sought establishment for over 2,500 years, wouldn't the best ideas already have obtained some reality by now? Wouldn't any remaining feasible improvements tend to be meager? If they were not meager but instead were important, why wouldn't they have gotten some establishment already? There are some threads of evidence that this idea of limitation can be relevant for societal progress, and we will now discuss some of these.

A. THE END OF HISTORY

Almost two decades ago, Francis Fukuyama developed his thesis in *The End of History*. This was a view that liberal democracy had developed in many countries in the twentieth century and that these countries had shown enough socio-political progress that it appeared that this is the best possible form of government. Eventually, this form of government would emerge everywhere and would prove to be the final and best form of government that mankind could contrive. Therefore, major changes in trying to improve types of governance essentially had come to an end.

Of course, such an antiprogressive idea would produce many criticisms in an age wherein very exuberant expectations of progress have become so ingrained. But some of the criticism of the end-of-history idea seems to naïvely assume that this phrase is to be taken very literally. In other words, the critics think Fukuyama is claiming a sharp and absolute end to all societal-historical change. Fukuyama surely is not claiming that all change is ceasing, rather that major developments in politics and governance will not be as pronounced or as fundamental as they sometimes have been. Certainly various events in the world will continue to happen, but such events do not compose the important historical evolutions upon which Fukuyama is focused. Fukuyama recognizes that the complete spread of liberal democracy will take considerable time. Essentially what he has said is that progress in enhancing modes of governance has entered well into the reverse-bending segment of the upper portion the sigmoid curve that I have previously discussed.

There are more meaningful criticisms of Fukuyama's thesis. Two important ones involve (1) radical Islamic fundamentalism as an alternative to governance by liberal democracy and (2) autocratic states such as Russia and especially China, which are becoming more capitalistic (as opposed to communistic) but are authoritarian-autocratic and not democratic. Many people fail to realize that communism fundamentally is an economic philosophy and not a system of governance; thus, authoritarian governments in Russia and China that developed under communistic philosophy could remain highly authoritarian and yet the economies could shift toward having some capitalistic qualities.

Fukuyama recognizes the argument regarding Islamic governments, but he feels they will eventually prove insufficient to permanently halt the spread of democratic liberalism, although the latter might take centuries. Questions regarding autocratic China and Russia are perhaps more problematic to speak to.

The important point for my purpose, however, is to note that even if Islamic-influenced or autocratic-capitalistic governments persist and Fukuyama ultimately is "proved wrong," such governments hardly seem to have any potential to be better than liberal democracies. In other words, socio-politico-economic progress for developed countries still seems to have entered into the limited reverse-bending portion of the famous sigmoid curve. This is pertinent to my ideas about scientific limitations perhaps having correlates for the humanities.

B. WORLD GOVERNMENT

Fukuyama's discussions are oriented mainly toward national governments. The question of the possibility of evolution of governance toward one big happy family of a united world still remains. Could liberal democracy progress to that extent? If so, that would be an amazing degree of social progress for us yet to see.

The tribal nature of man, evolving through a necessity for certain behaviors to enable survival, is so fundamentally ingrained that this idea doesn't seem very feasible. Man has an instinct to be wary of "other groups." Civilization can moderate this behavior to a degree, but disappearance of the instinct entirely would be highly unlikely. Uniting the world into one governance system would be a daunting challenge given the inevitable persistence of factions and regionalism. European nations have developed a union (the EU) that has some cooperative integration, but these nations have had some closeness generated by the long history of Western political, religious, and social philosophy that they share, and thus the union is still a very regional and limited union. And despite significant cooperation, the countries remain sovereign nation-states and the EU is far from being an effectively harmonious construct. It is doubtful that the union can foreshadow the development of a world government.

It is true that economic activities among various countries have changed in ways that are making the world seem more integrated. But this doesn't automatically translate into political integration. If one tries to discern progress toward world governance, one can examine the United Nations. If one looks there, clearly one will find naught in regard to such progress. This lack of progress is evidence that the idea of world governance almost surely is a utopian delusion.

Obviously the world is still built of nation-states and will remain so for an extremely long time. I can't predict the future in the long term, but anything like a single world governance would be so remotely in the future that for practical purposes of engaging in socio-politico-economic matters now, world governance cannot be part of our ideas about progress.

C. *Philosophy in the Modern World*

As evidence that progress in the humanities may have limits, just as science now seems to, we can make some comments about one of the most fundamental of humanistic endeavors, the "Long Debate," a term used by Daniel N. Robinson to refer to philosophy through the ages. It strikes me as a highly meaningful label because it portrays just how stubborn the great questions of philosophy are. Most of the big philosophical questions raised by the ancient Greeks are still being wrestled with during modern times. Perhaps these questions, or at least many of them, are irresolvable by limited man. If this is so, and the 2,500-year length of the continuing Long Debate suggests that it is, then this is some very profound evidence that socio-political progress—that is, improvement in governance—may be fundamentally limited. As Professor Robinson has pointed out, one of the three most all-encompassing, broad areas of philosophical inquiry can be subsumed under the label of problems of governance, including of course political science. The other two big areas are problems of knowledge—ontology and epistemology, which address what is real, what we can know, and how we know it—and problems of conduct, including ethics, morality, and how we should behave.

Since philosophical problems mostly seem so intractable, many people have tended to think that philosophy is essentially useless. I would point out, however, that philosophers at least describe and elucidate very fundamental problems that do exist and that affect us all. Just being able to make clear the problems that exist has value. "Philosophy is hard. It compensates us only with clarity, with the ability to see that the really deep problems resist solutions. But clarity is not just a cold comfort after all. As Bertrand Russell argued, it can be freeing. When things go well, philosophy can help us to see things that we wouldn't have been able to see or say otherwise" (J. L. Kasser). In the context of this book, philosophy can help us to see that socio-political-economic progress surely has some limits.

Modern liberalism certainly has fostered progress for much of Western society. But we may be starting upon the reverse-bending portion of the progress curve. This has major import for political-governmental decisions in the contemporary Western world.

D. *THE RELATIVISM OF POLITICAL ATTITUDES*

At its birth, the United States was swaddled in the best compilation of liberal ideas ever conjured. The political ideas of the federalists and the Constitution constitute the most magnificent combination of philosophical and pragmatic notions ever devised in the history of the world. These ideas were radically liberal at the time in that they rejected the long-standing (i.e., conserved) European history of governance based upon monarchial and theocratic-influenced societies of kings and churches.

The liberal democracy embodied in the Constitution can be called U.S. "classical liberalism." Our country has been built upon this foundation. This is what has been defended and preserved over two centuries by our country's best defenders. Gradually, these defenders came to be called "conservatives" because they struggled to preserve the best of the liberal basis for our country.

But a simultaneous gradual change has been the emergence of a powerful "progressive liberalism," becoming obtrusively prominent in the twentieth century. Progressive liberals are committed to efforts to continually change governance for the better. This would be a worthy goal if it were not for the looming of the reverse-bending part of the sigmoid curve of political progress. As time marches into the reverse-bending portion of the curve, progress becomes ever harder to achieve.

Thus, today's conservatives are yesterday's classical liberals. Today's liberals are "progressive liberals." Classical liberals are now conservative not because their fundamental ideas have changed but because the country has changed, or progressed. Relative to contemporary socio-political governance, what was radically liberal two centuries ago now is not judged as liberal but rather as conservative. Relativism works both ways, of course, and relative to contemporary conservative views, contemporary liberals seem hyperliberal, ultraliberal, and even utopian. This is what is meant by the relativism of political attitudes. The important question is, where do contemporary conservatives and progressive liberals stand relative to the best type of practical progress that can be made for our society?

E. Utopianism

The persistent optimism about progress that most Americans and many others currently maintain has over time developed a utopian quality. This is especially evident to a person like myself who has a sense of the limitations of progress. This utopian quality is particularly problematic when actually an opposite perspective is becoming increasingly important. A few words about utopianism are appropriate here.

The use of the word today comes mainly from a book by Thomas More, a work describing an imaginary land, possibly a large island not far from what is now Florida. The book was published in 1516 and is a rather complicated work, and scholars interpret More's possible aims in differing ways. It is clear that the aims involve political commentary, but the details of More's actual political beliefs are somewhat less clear. The commonly construed idea that Utopia was a perfect place is not quite correct. For example, divorce was very easily obtained (significant because More was Catholic), and euthanasia was practiced. Although slaves were "treated very well," slavery nevertheless was present in the land. The fact that Utopia was not quite perfect is an important point regarding our discussion because modern utopian goals based upon the ethos of unlimited progress often imply the goal of perfection. One should remember the original literal Greek meaning of the word "utopia." It means "no place," and thus the word ironically contains within itself the impossibility of the idea. Modern idealists should try to keep this in mind.

Thomas More was not the only person to espouse utopian ideals. Plato's *Republic*, the scholar's writings on governance, has a clearly utopian flavor. Karl Marx developed an economic philosophy that has proved to be very utopian. The disturbing fact is that current progressive liberalism seems to be heading unrelentingly in the utopian direction. This "progress" will end up going no place.

F. CONSERVATISM IS A MUST

It is probable that only diminishing returns can now be expected from continued socio-political change. This needs to be recognized, but it is not so by contemporary progressive liberals. A recent book *What's the Matter with Kansas?* is an example. The book has several flaws that have been criticized, and most of them are more important than the following point. But this point is relevant for our discussion. An undercurrent in the book indicates that the relativism of political attitudes and how they change over time has been ignored. Kansas became a territory in 1854 and then a state in 1860. It was a free state, that is, a non-slavery state, while next-door Missouri was a slave state. Major conflicts between these two adjacent states emphasized the radical liberal (at that time) nature of Kansas. The book's author looks at contemporaneous Kansas and perceives an ultraconservative quality, with some Kansans having become so conservative as to even vote against their own economic self-interest. The flavor underlying this implies that Kansas has regressed over the last century. What the author fails to realize is that since American society has progressed, Kansans could have either remained mostly the same or even progressed to some degree. It seems they have regressed only *relative* to overprogressive liberalism. For example, in 1860, Kansans who were against slavery seemed very liberal. Today, virtually all Kansans are against slavery, but this doesn't seem to count as liberal since Kansans don't stand out relative to the rest of the country in this regard.

Among numerous examples that could be chosen to further illustrate the relativism of political attitudes, the importance of labor unions in the economic life of the country is perhaps a good one. Capitalism can certainly develop problems, and harsh treatment of workers in the nineteenth century is one of them. In this earlier period, labor unions were important in bringing progress by working to end the maltreatment of laborers. But as this progress has occurred, labor unions have become increasingly less important. In this context, overly strong unions can cause problems that overshadow the good that they seek. An example would be the adverse effect that strong Teamsters unions have had on railroads, causing some regression of the effectiveness of rail transport. We need abundant trucks for commerce, obviously, but rail transport is much more efficient for long-distant transport of heavy freight. Trucks are required for local transport and delivery, but for long hauls they are inefficient compared to trains. It is true that train transport requires the extra steps of on-loading and off-loading from local truck transport that can be eliminated if trucks are used as the sole, one-step transport for long-distance hauling, but this minor inefficiency is dwarfed by the huge savings garnered with long-distance rail freight. Yet the Teamsters unions were a big factor in hamstringing freight trains via fostering the establishment of various regulative encumbrances in the middle part of the century. This disadvantage is now being realized, and trains will make a bit of a comeback largely because of the need for reducing greenhouse gas emissions from the huge number of trucks on the road.

As another example, the fact that United Auto Workers unions contributed to the recent problems of U.S. carmakers is recognized by most—albeit not all, of course—people. Thus, these labor union examples serve as evidence of how progressive liberal goals can be harmful when the relativism of the goals, and the consequent diminution of their importance over time, is ignored.

Having a conservative political viewpoint and attitude is thus becoming ever more important. This doesn't mean that political-governmental progress needs to completely stop. Useful change can still occur, but implementing change through political means needs to be done ever more circumspectly and cautiously. Changing things just for the sake of change, which tends to result from a utopian worldview, is more likely to have adverse, unintended consequences than it is to have value. Unfortunately, current political events obviously have been replete with overenthusiastic expectations from change. Change needs to proceed only with care and with a conservative outlook.

Of course, current conventional conservative views are not always perfect. This is particularly true in the economic realm with regard to *laissez faire* market ideas. Even Adam Smith, the primary voice for these ideas, recognized that absolute freedom of markets could result in some disadvantages. There are some hints in his philosophy that some management or regulation of capitalism is probably necessary. Current capitalism in the United States, whether during Democrat or Republican administrations, is "hooked on progress" (Robert Samuelson). In order for the economy to be maintained, it must grow and grow at exponentially increasing rates. The need for growing the economy is espoused by virtually all. Growth of the GDP is based on two things: increase in the number of workers and increase in the productivity of those workers. We are entering a period of decreased rate of growth of labor because of the aging of the baby boomers that will last a long time. Birth rates for most parts of the population are declining. There is evidence that productivity growth is slowing, and this is certainly not surprising to me since productivity progress almost surely has some sigmoid curve limits as does almost everything else.

Dependence on growth and the frailty engendered by such dependence can clearly be seen in the stock market if one looks at this market with any degree of realism. The birth of the market was based upon one source of return on investments: payments to investors from profits. But of course, our fantastic economic growth over the last two centuries has meant that the value of almost all stocks has increasingly been based upon their growth potential. This is true of so-called value stocks since the price-earnings ratios of most such stocks are very large numbers. And of course, many "growth stocks" have no earnings and pay no dividends. The fact that this house of cards has not only persisted but also grown tremendously over the two centuries is certainly no guarantee that it will persist into the indefinite future. Back-bending of a stock market progress curve could produce a catastrophe, not just a bear market, for our economy.

Thus, even conservatives may have to do better. In this context, which indicates big challenges even for conservatives, the utopianism of progressive liberals begins to take on an even more frightening flavor—extremely frightening.

G. The Pessimism of Conservatism

Conservatism is often considered by many to be pessimistic. It is. But it is a pessimism that can be tempered. Conservatism does not rule out progress; it just aims to serve progress that has a reasonable chance of being beneficial. In being so tempered, it becomes better labeled as "realism" rather than pessimism.

Sigmund Freud was a pessimist, as he freely admitted. Some of

Freud's views have been questioned in the latter twentieth century to the point that there has been a tendency to consider him to have been wrong. But the criticisms are mostly directed toward matters relative to his therapeutic psychoanalytic techniques. His broader viewpoints about man and society, expressed in his last major work *Civilization and Its Discontents,* show a profound understanding of the world, and the ideas are probably still very valid. The views are based upon a realistic view of human nature, and they tend to support the thesis that progress is limited. Such a pessimistic view will be considered by many as extremely negative, to the point of possibly being harmful. The many people who have great faith in the "power of positive thinking" certainly would hold this opinion. As Barbara Ehrenreich argued in her book *Bright Sided,* however, positive thinking can certainly be overzealous, and indeed it can become harmful in some ways. A somewhat pessimistic realism, a vigilant realism, often is necessary. Indeed, expecting a possible negative outcome was necessary for our survival in a more primitive state. If one is in the wild and detects movement of another creature nearby but doesn't clearly see the creature, it is better to have a pessimistic view that it is likely a predator. This is more realistic under the circumstances than to have an optimistic view that the creature is not a threat. If the optimistic view is wrong, there can be a sudden end of reality for the optimist.

The idea that conservatives are pessimistic and therefore necessarily comprise "The Party of No" will be addressed in the next chapter.

Chapter 12

The Positive Power of the Necessary Negative

The U.S. political party associated with conservatism, the Republican Party, is often disparaged by being referred to as the Party of No. Conservatives are often viewed as being obstructionist. The assumption underlying this criticism is, of course, that being negative and expressing a "no" is bad. It is assumed that this is retrogressive, that it counteracts progress. Perhaps surprisingly, this assumption is false.

Expressing a negative signal is much, much more important than expressing positive ones for maintaining some degree of order and for preserving anything resembling stability in the world. In order to thoroughly understand this assertion, it is necessary to review the absolute indispensability of feedback control for all kinds of systems in the world. In order to best explain feedback control, I will focus on physical or electromechanical technological systems, but I emphasize that similar notions have been applied to numerous sorts of socioeconomic systems. Certainly there is relevance for political systems also.

A. CYBERNETICS

The story begins with the development of the field of cybernetics in the 1940s. Norbert Wiener is remembered as the main contributor to the commencement of the development of the field, although there certainly were other contributors. Initial contributions in a 1943 publication partly authored by Arturo Rosenblueth are an example.

Most people today don't know the meaning of the word "cybernetics." This is peculiar considering the huge importance of cybernetics within so many aspects of our world. Almost everyone is familiar with the prefix "cyber" as used in the words "cyberspace" or "cyberworld," which refer to complex computer networks such as the Internet or the World Wide Web. The prefix used in this context, however, has a connotation that has been vastly altered from the original meaning. These altered meanings were partly derived from notions in a popular science fiction novel published in 1984 (*Neuromancer,* by William Gibson). The novelist coined the word "cyberspace."

"Cybernetics" derives from the Greek word *kybermetes,* meaning "steersman, pilot, rudder, or governor." We can envision a person steering a boat as an example of cybernetic control of a dynamic process. This will illustrate the meaning of cybernetics. In this example, the system of control includes the eyes and brain of the steersman, the hand of the steersman on the boat's rudder control mechanism, and the rudder. The input signal to this simple system is the direction and magnitude of the force from the steersman's hand. The output is the force altering the rudder direction. The feedback loop in this example is embodied in the steersman's eyes and brain. His eyes detect the disparity between the present heading (direction of travel) of the boat and the desired heading. When the boat starts to veer from the desired heading, the steersman's brain processes this information and sends an appropriate signal to his hand to correct the input force (information signal) that moves the rudder. This alters the rudder orientation in the appropriate direction and to the appropriate magnitude.

A very similar process occurs in an electromechanical device known as a servomechanism, often denoted just as "servo" for brevity. The servo consists of an electric motor with its rotatable armature being mechanically connected to some device, for example, an airplane elevator, which needs to be continually monitored and oriented in appropriate directions and magnitudes. The desired orientations are continually controlled by the servo. (Note that the servo motor armature does not continuously rotate as do the armatures in most applications for motors, but rather the armature rotates only the few degrees necessary to point the elevator in the desired direction.) This servo-controlled system can be represented as in Figure 8.

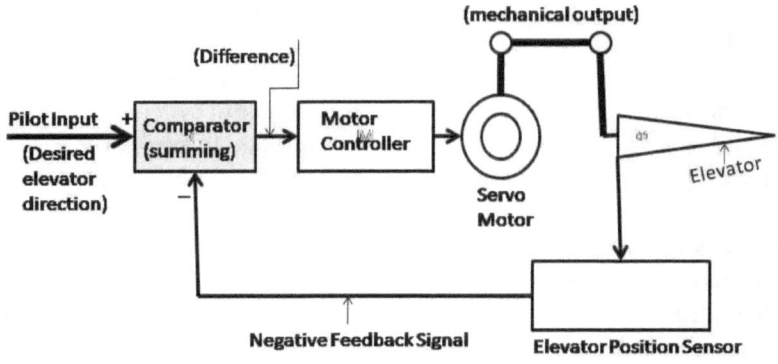

Servo Control of Airplane Elevator
Figure 8

The input signal to the system of Figure 8 is a voltage that, together with a current, powers the servomotor and moves the armature in the desired direction toward the desired elevator orientation. The armature is mechanically coupled to the elevator, and the elevator orientation is the system output. The feedback control portion of the system begins with a sensor device that monitors (senses) the present elevator orientation or direction. This direction is "fed back" and compared to the desired direction, and an error signal is produced. The production of the error signal is an information-processing step. Voltages represent both the present and desired elevator directions. One voltage is subtracted from another, resulting in the magnitude of error signal. This error signal is the result of information processing begun with the feedback signal, and it results in controlling the system toward the desired goal.

If the servomotor has moved the elevator too far in one direction or the other, the feedback signal must cause the motor to move in the reverse direction. In other words, whatever the input signal (voltage) was that resulted in moving the elevator to its present direction, that voltage must be reduced in order to modify the direction of the elevator toward the desired direction. The feedback voltage, therefore, must be in the negative polarity compared to the polarity of the extant input voltage. Thus, we are in the domain of *negative* feedback control. The polarity of the signal is the negative of the input voltage because this is what is required for system control.

There is also such a thing as positive feedback. But pure positive feedback results in uncontrolled and sometimes disastrous system outputs. When an input signal to a system causes an increase in system output, if the feedback signal is a positive one, this signal will augment the input signal and therefore cause a further increase in output. This will increase the magnitude of feedback, further increasing output. This is a "vicious circle" or "vicious cycle." What we then have is the famous exponentially increasing curve for the output. As mentioned in Chapter 3, this can result only in an explosion or other destructive outcome for the system.

We could also have a system wherein the input signal produced a decrease in output. In this system, positive feedback would increase the input, as with the prior system, resulting in a further decrease in output. This will lead not to an explosion but rather to zero output from the system. The system is dead. Of what use is such a system?

An example of the effect of a positive feedback process is the interference with an audio amplification system caused by reflected sound waves. When a speaker uses a microphone connected to an amplifier to address an audience, sometimes the amplified sound directed toward the audience can be reflected back toward the microphone with enough strength (amplitude or volume) that the microphone picks it up and sends it back through the amplifier. This bit of previously amplified sound is amplified again and then, being again partially reflected back toward the microphone, is again reamplified. This is uncontrolled positive feedback entering into the "vicious cycle." The result is the familiar horrendously loud, distorted, unusable noise. This is the sound of destructive wildness resulting from positive feedback, without the presence of modifying, controlling negative feedback.

B. CYBERNETICS BEYOND SERVOMOTORS

Physiologists have known about feedback control systems for more than a century. These systems maintain what is called homeostasis in the body. "Homeostasis" means a relatively steady state for such physiologic parameters as blood pressure, body temperature, pulse rate, and so on. It is not at all surprising that the body would have such negative feedback control circuits and networks because, as is being made clear by this discussion, the world is replete with systems that require such. But such control systems very often are subtle, and many times they escape notice. An example is the underrecognition of the importance of such control systems for higher brain functions. Neurophysiologists have long known about feedback control for some neural functions, for example, the nerve control of muscles. Also, the lower and middle brain is involved with control networks that include feedback loops, and this has been known for some time. Some homeostatic mechanisms just mentioned are of this type. But there has been only poor recognition of the extent of the involvement of higher (cortical) brain functions in top-down (i.e., directed toward lower brain structures) feedback functions.

For about two centuries, the picture of the organization of the brain that developed was one of information flowing from sense organs such as eyes and ears into the lower centers and then upward to the higher centers in the cortex. The cortex processed the information and then sent signals as necessary to peripheral parts of the body, such as muscles. But the importance of feedback signals to the lower brain centers and even to the level of inputs from sense organs for purposes of influencing, enhancing, and controlling the overall processing done by brain functions has been only poorly recognized. A middle brain structure named the lateral geniculate body is an early-stage processing center for signals coming from the retina on their way to the occipital visual cortex. The nerve channels leaving the geniculate and on their way "upward" are outnumbered ten to one by feedback channels going from the cortex back to the geniculate. These channels carry signals that are essentially negative feedback information for purposes of modulation and control. These influences clearly must be indispensable for proper brain function.

Neurons in the brain and elsewhere have a strong tendency to "fire" their impulses. They are almost always "itching" to go. They easily can become overactive if not properly monitored and controlled. This is probably an underlying cause of epileptic seizures. These attacks are a result of uncontrolled and chaotic firing of neurons in a region of the brain.

Arturo Rosenblueth knew in 1943 the very wide extent and

importance of negative feedback control. He indicated that behavior controlled by negative feedback—whether in animals, humans, or machines—was a determinative, directive principle throughout nature and human creations. Not surprisingly, in contemporary times, feedback control has been studied in fields such as economics and sociology. The application in these areas becomes complicated and sometimes confusing and controversial. This is because the human behavior underlying these fields is of course very complicated. One thing that should be pointed out is that the terms "positive feedback" and "negative feedback," when used colloquially in socioeconomic settings, have taken on meanings that are rather opposite to their meanings in technological contexts. Positive and negative feedback in social contexts refer, respectively, to praise and criticism. Thus, positive is good and negative is bad. This is really opposite to the implications of control in technical systems where negative feedback (control and maintenance) is good and positive feedback (usually loss of control and calamity and collapse) is bad.

If neurophysiologists can fall short of recognizing the extent of feedback control in the brain, one can imagine how hidden such processes are within socio-political systems. But one philosopher of science and sociological theoretician, Karl Popper, recognized how very important criticism is, both in science and humanities, for preventing errors in judging the validity of ideas. He also recognized how difficult it can be for people in various fields to accept and build upon criticism from others.

Criticism is very important, however, in politics and governance. Political change comes with risk. The risk is that the change may have unintended adverse consequences. Since progress is likely becoming ever more difficult to attain, the risk in making changes is tending to increase.

Conservatives are not against all change, but they are aware of the risks of change. Therefore, change has to be undertaken judiciously and with circumspection. Conservatives have their hands on the brakes of the train of progress. Since the risk of calamity to the train may be increasing, the brakemen are becoming more indispensable. A train traveling too fast for the prevailing conditions is headed for disaster. Since increasing the influence of the negative feedback control, or brakes, for the political progress train is becoming more important, it is now time for political independents to hop off the fence of indecisiveness, and we will examine the reasons for this in the next chapter.

Determining the exact methods for best achieving the practical application of control theory in a political context may be quite a challenge. But this should not cause us to lose sight of the underlying point of this chapter. Some kind of control needs to be involved in politics just as it is needed in all the many other systems of the world. And even though the exact details of how this control can best be achieved may remain fuzzy, the control must involve something analogous to negative feedback. Judicious constraints must be involved as political change is undertaken. Obviously, the political party most suited for accomplishing this control is the one with the most conservative flavor.

This does not mean that change in the direction of progress must grind to a halt. On the contrary, this is the only way that change can occur while remaining focused on the direction desired for the change. And tighter control over the direction of our ship of state is becoming increasingly necessary. This necessity arises from the increasing size of the utopian progressive liberal waves that batter the ship and are increasingly moving it off course. The altered course resulting from the uncontrolled, increasing waves is tending toward a heading for the ship that is directed at the rocks upon which the Utopian Sirens are singing. It is with this image in mind that we launch into the discussion in the next chapter as to why it is becoming crucial for political independents to jump off their fence of indecisiveness.

Chapter 13
Time for Independents to Fall Off the Fence

This chapter will be a bit different from previous ones in the following respect. In previous comments and discussions, I tried to include at least some of what can be considered as "evidence." That is, I have focused on objective or at least semi-objective facts, usually from the realm of science and technology. This chapter will be almost solely about political attitudes, and my comments should be viewed as only opinions rather than manifesting evidence for any claims. Nevertheless, the opinions are related to the prior evidence from scientific matters and in my view are of some importance.

The comments in this chapter are especially focused on the national level. If one looks at local or relatively small regional levels, there can be significant variations from region to region in political parameters. By "parameters," I mean such factors as the percentage of voters allied with a specific party, the importance of specific political issues, and so on. In a given small region, an issue that is of little importance on a national scale may be of much importance for the local voters. A minor political party that is of almost no importance nationally may have significant import for a small region.

When one considers, however, over a hundred million voters nationally, the local or regional variations tend to "average out" over the huge spectrum of national voters. Recall the simple ideas related to statistical sampling of a population. For a given measurement of some parameter in the population, say for example an opinion about a specific political issue, one can poll a sample from the population. If the sample is small, there can be a relatively large percentage error in the measurement of the opinion just from happenstance or chance variation. As the sample size becomes larger, however, the error tends to become relatively (i.e., percentage of sample size) smaller. The measurement expressed as the average of opinions becomes more reliable as a reflection of the true average opinion in the population as the sample size becomes larger. Likewise, minor issues that may be important in only a few localities are diluted, or "averaged out," on a national scale. This dilution also affects the relevance of minor political parties that may have some relevance on a regional level. On a national scale, these minor parties are diluted of any relevance.

It is now important for all voters to develop a more conservative viewpoint. In this context, I will argue why it is important—necessary, actually—for those who consider themselves as political independents to rethink this noncommittal attitude. Political independents are, of course, those voters who do not consider themselves definitely or formally allied with or a member of a political party. Independents have recently become an even bigger part of the electorate. Most Americans seem to be more pragmatic than ideological. This attitude is becoming increasingly disadvantageous for the well-being of the nation for reasons we will examine.

The most basic underlying reason is the one relating to the last chapter, the increasing importance for the necessary conservative brakes to be present in politics. But the relevance of independents to this assertion perhaps is not so obvious. I will try to explain its relevance.

We need to focus on the paramount importance of the two-party system in the United States. For the approximately 220 years of its governmental existence, the United States has had essentially only two political parties. For the last 155 years, it has very clearly been only two parties. It is true that there are and have been additional minor parties, but they have been so minor as to be unimportant, at least on a national level.

For the first sixty-five years, up until the founding of the Republican Party in 1854, the binary-party dynamic was less stable than subsequently and there were a few changes during this time. The most fundamental and disruptive change unfolded just prior to the Civil War. This was during a period of political chaos that was, of course, a result of the tumultuous slavery issue. The Whig Party was the progressive half of the political landscape, but the Whig leadership did not take a decisive stance on the slavery issue. This split the party along the north-south dividing line. The South aligned with the proslavery Democrat Party, while in the northern states, the increasingly active antislavery Republican Party rapidly evolved into the second major party, replacing the Whigs.

Since then, the Republicans and Democrats have constituted a very stable two-party system. The reasons for this are multiple, but one of the most important factors relates to a hypothesis or principle espoused by Maurice Duverger a half century ago. This principle is now known as Duverger's "law" and asserts that a "plurality rule" election system, versus a proportional representation or parliamentary system, favors the evolution of a two-party system. A plurality system marginalizes smaller political parties.

The reason this is so can be seen in the following example of an election occurring in a voting district. Assume there are 180,000 voters involved. The election is for a single official seat, and each voter has one vote. Three candidates are running. One candidate we can designate as radical, and the other two, while having some differences, can be described as moderates. The two moderate candidates have aligned themselves with two different moderate political parties, with each of these two parties having substantial membership.

Among the voters, 100,000 have moderate political views, and 80,000 have radical ones. Assuming that the voters all vote according to their predispositions, the radical candidate will win the election unless one of the moderate candidates receives fewer than 20,000 votes. A moderate voter, therefore, would be better advised to vote for the moderate candidate who is more likely to receive the larger number of votes, regardless of the moderate party with which the voter is more aligned. In other words, a moderate voter will be more satisfied with a moderate winner, even if that winner were his or her second choice, than with having the radical candidate win. This strategy would allow for the defeat of the radical candidate. Either the two moderate parties must merge into one or else one of the two must fail as moderate voters gravitate toward the stronger of the two moderate parties.

Duverger's law is still debated, and many argue that there are other factors relevant to the question of why we have a two-party system. Some point out historical factors. The country began with two parties, the Federalists and the Anti-federalists, the two being a reflection of the differing views of two very strong founding fathers, Hamilton and Jefferson. It can be argued that this very profound early binary polarization of our politics has had some persisting influence, some inertia as it were, on our party system.

Duverger himself admitted that his principle is not absolutely determinate by itself. The fact remains, however, that for 150 years, the United States clearly has had only two relevant parties. It is not important for our purposes to try to examine what minor influences might have contributed to this persistency. The important fact is that the two-party system is what we have. A third party might gain some temporary traction on a local level, but the United States is homogeneous enough on a broad national scale that two parties are here to stay for the foreseeable future. There will be no disruptive influence of the magnitude of the slavery issue. One can argue that there may be some disadvantages to the two-party system, but that is not relevant to our discussion. On a national level, including congressional seats, a voter absolutely must choose between Republican and Democrat candidates. (A so-called independent like Joe Lieberman cannot be considered an exception because his state's voters knew him so long as a Democrat.)

This is why the intrusion of third-party candidates into presidential elections is so idiotic. It is more than useless; it is harmful. The political views of a third-party candidate and the voters attracted to the candidate will be at least a bit closer to the views of one of the major-party candidates than to the other. This might be considered an oversimplified statement because the congeries of issues is complex and because what are considered the most important issues will vary from voter to voter. But on average, the statement has validity. The third-party candidate will surely draw voters away from the major party candidate who expresses views that are closer to those of the third-party candidate. This is clearly a self-defeating process. A minority-party candidate no doubt will argue that there are reasons for the candidacy. For example, it may be claimed that this is the only effective way to increase publicity for the candidate's views. It will be argued that the only way for a party to grow into a major power is to start somewhere, even if the start is a small one. These arguments are completely overshadowed by the importance of the disadvantages. The third party has no feasible chance of growing into a major party. The historical evidence indicates this to be so.

The fact that a third-party candidate can be—actually, certainly will be, at least to some degree—a "spoiler" is well known. I emphasize it here, however, because it has not been given its due degree of importance. This is especially important in the context of the thesis of this book. There are only two parties of national import, and this will persist. Therefore, a voter must choose a candidate from one of these two. It frequently is pointed out that being conservative is not the same as being a Republican and being liberal is not identical with being a Democrat. But when national voting time comes, they should be. Even though some conservatives are disappointed with the Republican Party at any given time, they have no other rational choice but to vote for the Republican candidate. If a conservative is unhappy with the party that is closest to his or her conservative attitude, the only thing to be done is to try to do something within the party context to alter the views, attitudes, or policies within the party in the desired directions.

There is now an increasing tendency for voters to consider themselves moderate and independent. They emphasize that their vote will be cast after careful consideration of the details of a candidate's views on the various specific issues. This will be argued as being politically astute and the only way for an intelligent voter to behave. It may be true to some degree on a local level. But on a national level, it is not. Even if a voter is middle-of-the-road on most issues, he or she will be at least a bit closer to being either conservative or liberal-progressive in basic political philosophy. The voter should realize the importance of this and orient his or her voting toward one party or the other.

Independent voters often are greatly influenced by personal qualities of candidates, that is, how they look, how they speak, and so on. These personal qualities cause them to "like" one candidate over the other, and they may claim that this is the only sensible way to be. This is understandable, and it is a very basic human behavior. It is a very human way of making judgments about other people, and for most purposes, it is the most effective way. Again, on a local political level, it may maintain some legitimacy. On a national level, however, it should be consciously resisted or at least mitigated. The party in power on a national level has tremendous power and advantage for influencing the political dynamics of the country. A voter needs to have some faith that the party's choice for a national candidate has enough validity to override any concern on the part of the voter about some personality trait that might seem disturbing. A voter needs to consciously train himself or herself to think differently when voting nationally versus when voting locally.

Political polls suggest that in the group of independent voters, there is a bias toward moderate conservatism. Thus, if members of this group get off the fence, conservatism will probably benefit, which is becoming ever more important. The nation needs the temperate feedback control that conservatism might be able to exert on the uncontrolled, irrational exuberance of liberal-progressive utopianism.

The last election and subsequent affairs illustrate this unfortunate state of affairs. The giddiness of the prospect of change became so dominant that there was a clear tendency to favor change for change's sake, with no significant thought given to the risks brought with this attitude. The disastrous health care bill is an example of an adverse effect from this attitude. The effort to reform health care became dominated by the need to just get something passed by the end of the year regardless of what it was. In other words, the progressive-liberal need was to get some kind of change on the books regardless of what the effects of this change would be. If ever a piece of legislation needed the negative feedback control of conservatism, this was a prime example. Of course, conservatives gave feedback a good try, but there were too few conservatives in Congress. My head aches as I think about this fiasco.

The world needs to start adjusting to the new reality, the reality that the rate of feasible progress cannot keep increasing. There are limits. I've given you evidence.

Commentator Evan Thomas remarked that history is filled with examples of political leaders of nations who, in retrospect, probably made very bad choices for their nations in times of turmoil or major challenges for their nations. Somehow, however, such nations usually "muddled through" the difficulties. History is mostly that of muddling through challenges rather than making the best decisions to confront difficulties. America will probably continue to muddle through problems in the future, at least in the near or middling future. Some muddles are, however, very difficult, agonizing, long, hard slogs through a lot of mud. Our slogs may increasingly be through mud that is mixed with significant amounts of progressive-liberal dung. If conservative efforts can decrease the amount of dung just a little, it will probably be worth the efforts.

Many will say that accepting this argument will increase the divisiveness of strong partisanship and will make it more difficult for government to make changes. Well, yes, and this will be a good thing. If a particular proposed item of change really is worthwhile, it will receive its due bipartisan support and will come about. If a proposed change is dangerous, conservative party allegiance will help ensure that we maintain the feedback control required for preventing runaway trains driven by the delusion of unlimited progress.

Acknowledgments

Some of the ideas expressed in Chapters 6, 8, and 9 were originally presented in the following published articles that were used in a different context and for a different purpose (for a medical readership):

(1) Heffner, D. K. Chaotic tumors and 2 mistakes of molecular oncologists. *Annals of Diagnostic Pathology*, 2005; 9:61–67.

(2) Heffner, D. K. Pathologists are from Mercury, clinicians are from Uranus: the perverted prospects for perceptual pathology. *Annals of Diagnostic Pathology*, 2008; 12:304–309.

(3) Heffner, D. K. Will a computer (with artificial vision) replace the surgical pathologist (or other health professionals)? *Military Medicine*, 1994; 159:A20–A26.